HOBBY HANDBOOKS™

STAMPS

MICHAEL BRIGGS

RANDOM HOUSE 🏠 NEW YORK

ACKNOWLEDGMENTS

Most of the photographs in this book were specially taken for the Octopus Publishing Group by David Johnson—the stamps were supplied by Stanley Gibbons Ltd or from the author's collection, unless otherwise credited below. The publishers would like to thank Tristan Brittain of Stanley Gibbons Ltd for the loan of the Irish £1 forgery on page 51; Malcolm Sprei of M&S Stamps, 77 The Strand, London, for the propaganda forgery on page 50; Stanley Gibbons Ltd, 399 The Strand, London, for the equipment, albums, and catalogs on pages 14-21 and 24; and the following individuals and organizations for permission to reproduce the pictures in this book:
Ancient Art & Architecture collection/Ronald Sheridan 54 top left.
Stanley Gibbons Ltd 32 top, 33, 46 top left and right, 47 top left, right, and center, 49 center, 50 bottom, 52 top, 53 top left, 54 right, 54-55, 56 upper and lower center, 56 bottom, 57 top and upper center, 59 bottom left, 62 top and bottom right, 64 top left, 65 top, 65 upper and lower center left. French Picture Library/Barrie Smith 11 bottom center, 12 top and bottom.
Magnum/Erich Lessing 55 bottom left; Mann Hughes Gerrish Ltd/Royal Mail Stamps 68.
National Postal Museum, London/Othens 49 top right, 50 upper and lower center, 62 lower center, 62 bottom left. Judy Todd 11 bottom left. John Walmsley 9 bottom right. ZEFA 11 top left, center and right, 11 bottom right, 13 left and right.

Illustrators:
Peter Bull Art: maps (72-75). David Ashby (Garden Studio): all other diagrams and artwork

First American edition, 1993

Manufactured in Great Britain 1 2 3 4 5 6 7 8 9 10

HOBBY HANDBOOKS is a trademark of Random House, Inc.

Briggs, Michael. Stamps / Michael Briggs. — 1st American ed. p. cm. — (Hobby handbooks) Includes index.
Summary: Provides information on the history of stamps and postal services and gives advice on identifying, handling, displaying, buying, and trading stamps.
1. Postage stamps—Collectors and collecting—Juvenile literature. [1. Postage stamps—Collectors and collecting.] I. Title. II. Series. HE6215.B65 1993
769.56—dc20 92-17278
ISBN 0-679-82664-5 (trade). — ISBN 0-679-92664-X (lib. bdg.)

CONTENTS

STAMP COLLECTING

Stamp collecting is one of the most popular hobbies in the world. Nobody knows for sure how many collectors there are. According to a United States Postal Service survey, 22 million people in the U.S. collect stamps in some way. Many of them just buy new issues that appeal to them.

THE FIRST OF MANY

The first adhesive postage stamp was issued by Great Britain in 1840 as a convenient way of showing that postage had been paid by the sender of a letter. In 1847, the United States issued its first adhesive postage stamps, which bore the portraits of George Washington and Benjamin Franklin. Franklin was the first U.S. postmaster general.

STAMPS AROUND THE WORLD

The idea of the postage stamp soon caught on in other countries as well. It was not long before people began to collect these tiny, usually exotic, pieces of paper from distant parts of the world. By the 1860s, famous names such as Stanley Gibbons in England, John Scott in the U.S., and Theodore Champion in France began to trade in stamps and to produce the first albums and catalogs. Stamp collecting captured the imagination of young and old, the ordinary and the famous: President Franklin Delano Roosevelt of the U.S. and King George V of Great Britain were avid collectors.

Today, collectors have a huge choice, because many hundreds of stamps are issued each year by almost every country in the world. Stamps provide a fascinating insight into many cultures, depicting landscapes and buildings, sports, wildlife, transport, art, and scientific achievement, among other things. Many, many subjects have appeared on stamps. All of this is captured on tiny pieces of paper, many of which are works of art in themselves.

Stamp dealer Theodore Champion and stamp production are shown on these two stamps (left).

STUDYING STAMPS

It is not until you begin to study stamps closely, to ask why and how they were produced, that you can call yourself a philatelist. A philatelist is someone who studies stamps, rather than just collects them. (The word *philately*, meaning "stamp collecting," is derived from the Greek word *ateles*, meaning "tax-free.") You can study the stamps of a single country, discovering why they were issued and how they were printed. Or you can delve into a country's postal history. Whatever you start to collect, you will soon discover why stamps have such worldwide appeal.

A Swedish stamp booklet (top) shows some of the many ways of transporting mail. The booklet from the U.S. (above) promotes a stamp exhibition—an ideal place to buy, see, and learn about stamps.

Postal history (above) and stamp collecting (above right) are popular subjects for stamps.

STAMP COLLECTING

You can devote as little or as much time to stamp collecting as you wish. Of course, chances are you won't be able to collect some of the more expensive or rare stamps, but this shouldn't reduce your enjoyment of the hobby. As with any activity, there is no substitute for help and guidance from experienced collectors. This book should help point you in the right direction. It is also worthwhile to join a local stamp club. Most experienced philatelists are only too pleased to advise young collectors.

Many collectors like to buy stamps by mail because it gives them more time, at home, to decide what they want for their collection. Never be hasty when looking at stamps. Sometimes you will find interesting postmarks or stamped messages on the envelopes.

WHERE TO OBTAIN STAMPS

You may have started to collect stamps when someone gave you a packet of them or a starter pack as a present. Perhaps you were attracted by colorful stamps on letters sent by friends from overseas. However you began, you will soon want to add to your collection, to fill gaps in a set, or to start collecting stamps of a new country. There are many ways of doing this.

STAMP PACKETS
Packets of stamps are widely available. They range in content from just a few stamps from a single country or subject to packets containing many hundreds of stamps from around the world. Packets are ideal for starting a collection—whether a general one, one on a single country, or one on a theme or subject—because you can obtain a large number of stamps, usually all different, quite inexpensively.

KILOWARE
Buying kiloware, a quantity of stamps cut from their envelopes and sold together by weight, is another way to begin a collection. Usually sold unsorted, kiloware can contain some scarce stamps, though there is a much greater chance of finding more common ones, as well as some damaged and heavily postmarked copies. You will need to sort the stamps carefully and prepare them by floating off the backing paper (see page 20) before mounting them in your album. Kiloware is also likely to contain many duplicate stamps: these can be traded with your stamp-collecting friends—yet another way to obtain stamps.

Stamp packets (above) and kiloware (below) are easy ways of building up a stamp collection.

STAMP DEALERS

If you are lucky enough to have a stamp store near your home, you can easily go there and look at the dealer's stock. You will be able to obtain advice there as well. Stamp fairs are held in many places, either on a regular basis or perhaps as a special event organized by the local stamp club. You will find at least half a dozen stamp dealers, offering a wide choice of material, at these fairs.

Many stamp dealers sell by mail: a glance through one of the monthly stamp magazines available at your newsstand or local library will reveal dealers offering everything from cheap packets and sets to rare, and expensive, single stamps.

Stamps can also be sent to you "on approval." Just select and pay for those you have decided to buy and return those you don't want.

LOOKING AT POSTAL HISTORY

Postal history is the study of all aspects of a postal system and its development. It forms an important background to stamp collecting and has many fascinating sidelines. For example, mailboxes—the first roadside mailbox for the collection of letters was introduced in Paris in 1653—can be found in many different styles. There is even a club for those who are interested in them. Some unusual boxes from around the world are shown below.

A box from Budapest, Hungary.

This ornate box is from Germany.

A wall box from the Faroe Islands.

A modern French box with one slot for local and one for long-distance letters.

An Indian pillar box.

This two-slot box is from Hong Kong.

POST OFFICES

If you collect stamps of your own country, one important source is your local post office. Many larger post offices have a special section devoted to the needs of collectors, though you will, of course, only be able to buy new and recent issues there. You also may want to write to the U.S. Postal Service, Philatelic Sales Division, Customer Services, Box 449997, Kansas City, Missouri 64144-9997. Most overseas post offices, too, provide a postal service for collectors (see page 69).

STAMP CLUBS

All serious stamp collectors should belong to a stamp club. Turn to page 68 for information on the different types of clubs and the advantages of membership. A major advantage is the opportunity to exchange stamps with fellow members. Many clubs run an "exchange packet" through which members can sell their stamps. The packet (a page from a book) is passed from one person to the next, by hand or by mail. This gives those unable to attend meetings regularly a chance to buy and sell stamps.

Stamp vending machines (right) often provide stamps that cannot be bought at the post-office counter. The machine from the U.S. (right) has a wide choice of stamps. The Danish machine (far right) is located next to a mailbox; it sells stamp booklets.

COLLECTOR'S HINT
Don't forget to take your tweezers when you go to a dealer. A pocket stockbook in which to keep your purchases and a magnifying glass will be useful, too.

You can buy stamps at post offices (above). Many have special sections for collectors. Street markets, too, are a source of stamps; some, like this French one (right), are devoted just to collectors' needs.

EXHIBITIONS

Stamp exhibitions provide an excellent opportunity to buy stamps from a wide range of dealers gathered together under one roof. Small exhibitions are held throughout the country and are advertised in stamp magazines and locally. Larger, national shows are held, too. For example, Stampex is held twice a year in London (spring and autumn). Usually a hundred or more dealers attend.

On an even larger scale are the Internationals. Collectors from all over the world display their stamps, and many postal administrations and stamp dealers attend, too. For example, the 1986 AMERIPEX Show, held in Chicago, attracted more than 150,000 collectors from around the world.

AUCTIONS

There is another method of obtaining stamps: the stamp auction. Auctions range from those containing inexpensive sets and single stamps to those selling valuable specialized collections. All auctions have a catalog describing the lots (items) available and giving an idea of how much money they are expected to go for. The catalogs also provide details on how to bid. Collectors do not have to attend an auction in person, because bids can be placed by mail. Most auctions are for experienced collectors only.

BUYING STAMPS

Keep an up-to-date list of the items you want for your collection. Without one, it is very easy to buy a stamp that you already own.

Examine stamps and envelopes carefully before you buy them. Check for small tears, missing perforations, staining, and other damage.

Don't forget to look at the backs of stamps, especially if buying unmounted ones. Faults often show up better from the back of a stamp than from the front.

ALBUMS

It is not until your stamps are sorted and arranged in some sort of order that they become a proper stamp collection. The easiest way to do this is to keep them in a stamp album.

PRINTED ALBUMS

The simplest type of album contains pages with printed headings for each country. Some have their pages bound like a book; others have loose leaves, allowing you to add pages as your collection grows.

Sooner or later, if you collect stamps from the whole world, you will decide to concentrate your collection on the stamps of just one country or area. If you are a one-country collector, you can choose to use one of the many printed albums available. They have a printed space for each stamp issued. All you need to do is to mount the stamp in its place. However, you will probably find that there are some spaces you will never fill.

BLANK ALBUMS

For most serious collectors, the blank loose-leaf album is the best choice. This contains pages printed with a faint grid to help you arrange your stamps. There are many different types and sizes of albums available: the larger ones are better for displaying blocks and longer sets of stamps.

Albums with blank pages enable you to arrange your collection just as you want. You don't have to follow any particular arrangement, and you can include whatever written information you wish. A blank album is almost essential for a person who collects topics rather than countries.

Leaves, or pages for the albums, should be chosen with care. Shiny, soft paper may tear when a stamp is removed, so a smooth, hard surface is better. Some leaves have a transparent paper leaf over them. This helps protect the stamps from damage.

OTHER ALBUMS

Special albums are made to hold first-day covers, postcards, and stamp booklets. These have leaves of transparent plastic pockets to protect the items. Stockbook-type albums contain pages with transparent strips attached to them. The stamps are placed behind the strips. There is no need to use a stamp hinge or protective mount. Pages with different numbers and sizes of strips are available, allowing items of various sizes to be held safely. A small stockbook is handy for holding your duplicate stamps or for stamps waiting to be mounted in your album.

Blank looseleaf albums (left) allow you to mount stamps as you wish and to include notes and other items in your collection. Printed albums (below left) are better for beginners or for straightforward collections.

COLLECTOR'S HINT
Never put too many pages in an album, especially a springback type, because the binding mechanism could be weakened. Always store your albums upright, not on their sides.

TYPES OF ALBUM

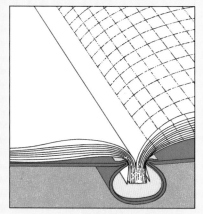

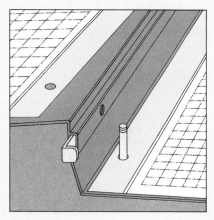

The traditional album binder is the springback. A concealed spring in the spine holds the leaves in place. One disadvantage is that the leaves do not lie flat when the album is open: they need to be removed when you are working on the collection. The leaves are removed by folding back the cover against the spring.

The peg-fitting album holds punched leaves on two pegs. It has a locking mechanism that secures the binder cover to the pegs. Like the springback album, the leaves do not always lie completely flat when the album is open. Leaves hinged with a linen cloth are sometimes used to make the pages lie flatter.

Perhaps the album most popular with collectors is the ring binder. The number of rings varies from two to twenty-two. Albums with lots of rings are best, as the pages are less likely to tear away from the binding rings. The pages will lie flat wherever the album is opened, and they can be removed very easily.

EQUIPMENT

Stamp collecting requires very little equipment. However, a few items other than albums and catalogs *are* essential to proper collecting. These basic items are readily available from stamp shops or by mail order from magazines. They need not be expensive.

MAGNIFYING GLASS

A magnifying glass allows you to examine the fine detail of a stamp's design, detect errors and varieties, and sometimes identify methods of printing. A wide range of magnifying glasses is available, from large hand-held types to small folding versions that fit easily into your pocket. Their magnification varies, too, so try out a few different glasses to see which is best for your needs—a fairly low-powered glass is suitable for most work. Choose one that gives a clear, undistorted field of view.

TWEEZERS

Stamps are fragile and can easily be damaged if you pick them up with your fingers. Tweezers, the stamp collector's most important tool, allow you to handle your stamps without fear of damage. Many types of tweezers are available, from fine rounded points to broad "spade" ends. Choose the type that suits you best. Make sure, however, to buy a pair intended for use with stamps. Using tweezers may seem difficult at first but should become easier with time.

PERFORATION GAUGE

A stamp's value may be increased if its perforation—the tiny holes around its edge used as a means of separating one stamp from another—is different from normal. A perforation gauge measures these differences. The perforation number is found by counting the number of holes that occur every 2 centimeters. By matching the perforations on the stamp with the dots on the card or plastic gauge, you can find the correct perforation measurement. These gauges usually give measurements as small as half a perforation. A more complex gauge is printed with fine lines instead of dots and measures more precisely.

USING A PERFORATION GAUGE

Align the perforation holes on the stamp with the dots on the gauge: when they match, you have the correct measurement. Most gauges show measurements as small as half a perforation. You should round up other fractions: for example, a measurement of between 13 and 13½ is rounded up to 13½.

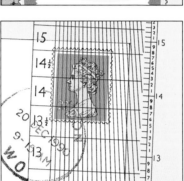

This gauge allows you to obtain a more precise measurement. The stamp is moved down the gauge until the lines cut through the centers of the perforation holes; the numerals on the right give the stamp's perforation. A transparent gauge lets you measure stamps that are still on an envelope or mounted in your stamp album.

A stamp with the same measurements on all four sides (say 13) is said to be perf 13. Often the top and bottom measurements are different from those at the sides, in which case the top measurement is given first. Perf 14 x 15, for example, means a measurement of 14 at the top and bottom and 15 at the sides.

COLLECTOR'S HINT
You can save time and effort when measuring the perforations of a lot of stamps by comparing them with a stamp that has already been measured. Use the perforation gauge to measure any that do not match.

OTHER EQUIPMENT
In stamp shops and in magazines you will see some other equipment for sale. While none of the items shown here are particularly expensive, only experienced collectors really need to buy them.

WATERMARK DETECTORS
Just as a difference in perforation can change the value of a stamp, so can a difference in watermark. A watermark is a deliberate thinning of the paper during its manufacture to form a design or pattern. This acts as a security device, because it makes stamps more difficult to forge.

Watermarks can often be seen by holding the stamp to the light or by placing it face down on a dark surface. But since many modern stamps are printed on thick, coated paper that makes the watermark difficult to see, various watermark detectors are available. Some of them even make it possible to find a watermark on a stamp still stuck to its envelope.

PEN AND STENCIL
Although not essential to a stamp collector, a lettering stencil and pen can be useful for adding neat notes to your collection.

COLOR GUIDES
Variations in the color of a stamp can also make a difference in its value. Trying to judge between different shades without help can be very difficult; a color guide is often useful.

Some guides are like a paint chart, although a better type has the colors printed on narrow strips of cardboard, like a fan. A hole punched through each color means the fan can be placed over the stamp for easy matching. Working in good daylight from a north-facing window is best for accurate color matching.

ULTRAVIOLET LAMPS

An ultraviolet (UV) lamp can be useful in detecting the phosphorescent inks and papers used on many stamps. Bands of almost invisible phosphorescent ink aid the sorting of mail by machine, because the machines are set up to detect the position of the phosphorescence. These bands can often be seen by holding the stamp at a slight angle against a light source, but a UV lamp makes their detection much easier. You will need to be an experienced philatelist before you require a UV lamp. Skill is needed in knowing what to look for, and great care must be taken in using a lamp—looking directly at UV light can damage your eyes very seriously.

WATERMARKS AND BANDS

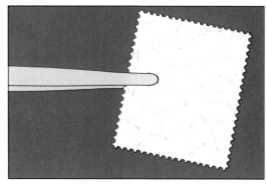

Some watermarks show up well on a dark surface or when the stamp is held up to the light. Before trying to detect watermarks, use a stamp catalog to give yourself an idea of the patterns you are looking for.

Holding a stamp at a slight angle to a light source can reveal phosphor bands. They show up as dull strips on the stamp's surface.

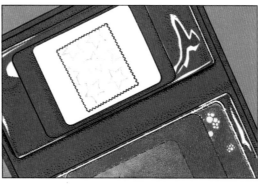

If simple methods fail to reveal the expected watermark, try using a watermark detector. First place the stamp facedown on the glass block. Then place the small plastic bag over it. The bag contains a special blue liquid.

Applying pressure to the plastic bag reveals the watermark as a pattern in the liquid. It will probably take a little practice before you become accustomed to using a detector like this.

CARE
OF
STAMPS

Since stamps are easily damaged, they should be treated with care. Always use stamp tweezers when handling them. Unless they are very rare and unusual, stamps that have been torn, creased, or stained, and those that are heavily postmarked, should be thrown away. They have no value and will spoil the appearance of your collection.

PREPARING STAMPS

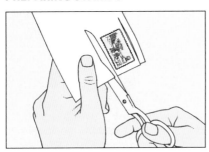

Unless you wish to keep the postmark intact, stamps cut from envelopes should be removed from the paper before being mounted in your album. First, cut the paper close to the stamps.

Next, put some warm water in a bowl and float the cut stamps on the surface of the water *stamp side up* until the backing separates from the stamps. Remember, wet stamps are very fragile.

It may take some time for a stamp's gum to become wet enough for it to separate from the paper. Do *not* be tempted to give a helping hand by pulling the paper from the stamp.

A stamp may still have some of its original gum on the back. Gently wash it off with a clean paint brush dipped in clean, warm water. Stamps should be placed on clean white blotting paper or on a kitchen towel to dry.

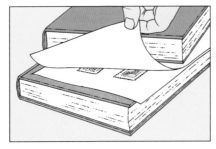

Let the stamps dry naturally, away from strong heat. They might curl slightly while drying. It is best to press them carefully between two sheets of blotting paper placed between a couple of heavy books, *after* they have dried.

COLLECTOR'S HINT
When floating stamps, put those on colored envelopes to one side. These should be treated separately in case the color runs when the piece is immersed in the water.

Stockbooks are useful for storing stamps. Keep your stockbook and albums in a clean, dry place.

MOUNTING STAMPS

Once prepared, your stamps can be mounted on your album pages with stamp hinges. These are small, gummed pieces of transparent paper made for this purpose. When dry, they can be peeled off both the page and stamp without damaging either one. Never be tempted to use other forms of adhesive paper, because you will damage your stamps. An alternative method, ideal if you do not wish to disturb the gum on the back of a stamp, is to use a protective mount. The stamp is slipped between two pieces of plastic that have been welded together on one or two sides. When the mount is stuck to the album page, the stamp remains fully protected. Protective mounts come either in strips to cut to the size you require or already cut to fit standard stamp sizes.

If you are not ready to mount your stamps, store them in a stockbook. These come in many sizes and have strips on each page. The stamps are held safely behind the strips until they are needed.

USING PROTECTIVE MOUNTS

Protective mounts are used for displaying mint stamps, whose value might be reduced by hinging them. Mounts are available in black and clear forms.

Protective mounts are stuck in the album by moistening their gummed backs. A small paper cutter makes cutting strips quick and accurate.

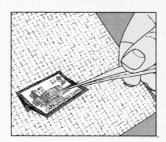

This mint stamp is being inserted into a double-sealed mount. Although protective mounts cost more than hinges, it is wise to use them for displaying mint stamps.

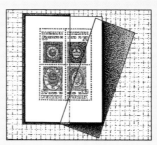

Two strips can be overlapped to mount large items and hold them securely. Photograph corners can be used to hold first-day covers.

USING A STAMP HINGE

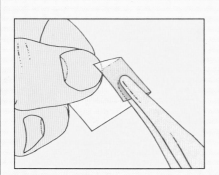

Fold over a third of the hinge, gummed side out. Some hinges are sold already folded.

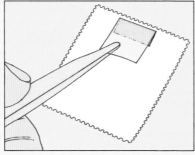

Lightly moisten the smaller portion of the hinge and place it at the top of the stamp.

Moisten the lower part of the free end of the hinge and place the stamp in position on the album page.

DISPLAYING STAMPS

How you arrange your stamps, and what additional information you include on the page, will depend on the kind of collection you are forming. Whether your collection is a simple "one of everything" type, highly specialized, or topical, it should be neat and organized.

Stamps

𝕾𝕿𝕬𝕸𝕻𝕾

STAMPS

Stamps

Stamps

Chagall : The Married Couple of the Eiffel Tower

Seurat : The Circus

Toulouse-Laut du 'Star

Braque : The Messenger

Cezanne : The Card Players

De La Fresnaye : 14th July

Dufy : The Red Violin

Rousseau : The Cart of Père Juniet

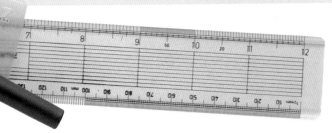

WRITING

Most blank album pages are printed with a faint grid to help you arrange your stamps. The grid also helps keep any writing straight and neat. But writing should be kept to a minimum. The stamps must be the most important items on the page. Keep any notes and labels small, and make sure they can be read easily.

Writing is best done with a fine-point pen. Use black ink, because this always looks best. Do not use a ballpoint, because the ink could form blobs that will smudge across your stamps. Stencils or a typewriter are other methods you might prefer to use. Experiment until you find what suits you best.

DESIGNING THE PAGE

Before mounting your stamps or beginning to write anything, arrange the stamps loosely on the page. Move them about until you get a pleasing display, remembering to leave space for any writing. Then mark the positions of the stamps very lightly with a pencil and add any written information. You are now ready to mount the stamps in their marked positions.

Most collectors keep to a symmetrical arrangement: the left side of the page matches the right side. Nevertheless, topical displays—which often contain stamps of different shapes and sizes as well as covers, postmarks, and other items—often look better without such a formal style. In country collections, sets of stamps are usually arranged in value order, though it is sometimes necessary to break this order to make a balanced page, especially if they contain different shapes and sizes. Arranging your stamps on an album page can be a very rewarding job. A neat and well-organized collection will give great pleasure to you and others who see it.

These French-art stamps are arranged symmetrically. They are mounted neatly on the page with enough space for a brief caption beneath each stamp. The other page is not so neat—the stamps are not straight.

COLLECTOR'S HINT
A simple ruler handmade from a strip of cardboard can help you locate a page's center or other points easily and quickly. This is a great help in positioning stamps.

PLANNING THE PAGE

Before you mount your stamps, arrange them loosely on the page, leaving space for any writing.

Once you like the arrangement, mark the stamps' positions with a light pencil dot by each of their corners.

After you write any notes on the page, you can mount the stamps in place.

CATALOGS

A stamp catalog is an essential item in the stamp collector's "tool kit," because it gives details on why and when stamps were issued. It shows you what other stamps you need for your collection and gives you an indication of what they will cost.

TYPES OF CATALOG

There are many types of catalogs available. They may, like Stanley Gibbons' *Stamps of the World*, provide a listing of stamps that differ only in appearance, ignoring such things as watermarks and any differences in perforations. Others provide more details, listing all possible stamp variations as well as providing other useful information such as a stamp's designer and printer.

Catalogs may cover a geographic area, such as Central America, or a single country. Thematic subjects such as birds, railroads, and ships also have their own catalogs. Most major stamp catalogs, such as the Scott catalogs, are published at regular intervals, and some have supplements to keep the listings up to date. Information about new issues of stamps can be found in stamp magazines.

USING A CATALOG

Always read the introduction to a stamp catalog. This will tell you what sorts of stamps are included. Most catalogs, for example, list only stamps issued by government postal administrations; privately produced stamps are not included. Sometimes stamps that have been issued just for collectors and serve no real postal need are listed in a special section. The introduction is also likely to explain about perforations, papers, watermarks, and other items of a technical nature.

All catalogs are well illustrated. Some show just one stamp in a set, others show all the designs within a set. The illustrations, together with brief descriptions of the stamps' designs, make it possible to find the stamp you are looking for. The number beside each listed stamp is the catalog number. This number serves as a convenient way of referring to a stamp without having to describe it in full.

COLLECTOR'S HINT
Dates are often included in stamp designs. These can be a great help in finding stamps in the catalog, especially if the country has issued many stamps.

Every collector needs a stamp catalog. There are many types available. Shown here are catalogs from Great Britain (Stanley Gibbons), the U.S. (Scott), Germany (Michel), and France (Yvert et Tellier).

USING A CATALOG

Catalogs have illustrations and descriptions to help you find the stamp you are looking for. The stamps are usually listed in order of their date of issue, although each catalog has its own numbering system.

The number on the left is the "catalog number." This is a simple way of describing a stamp. The stamps on this page are France 526 to 533.

The face value of the stamp.

Footnotes guide you to stamps in the same series.

Catalog illustrations are often in black and white. The stamp's main colors are described.

The figures at the right show the catalog prices for mint (unused) and used stamps respectively.

The design-type number can be useful for identifying the illustration of a stamp.

The perforation of the stamp.

The date of issue of the stamp.

1970-**72. Various issues with phosphor bands on stamps' faces.**
Perf 14 x 13½ (10c), 14 x 13 (30c) or 13 (others).

526	10c. Yellow, brilliant blue, and brown-red (three bands)	12	12
527	20c. Multicolored (three bands)	12	12
528	30c. Emerald (one band)	15	5
529	40c. Cherry (two bands)	3.50	1.50

Starting in March 1970, Nos. 526-29 were issued for use with automatic sorting machines that could separate the items of fast and slow mail. The phosphor bands react to long-wave ultraviolet light with a yellow or orange glow. *See also Nos. 556 and 568.*

1970, 21 March. *412.* **150th anniversary of the discovery of quinine.**
Designed and engraved by C. Haley. Recess. Perf 13.
530 50c. Deep green, light blue-green, and magenta 25 15

1970, 21 March. *413.* **European Nature Conservation Year.**
Designed and engraved by Cami. Recess. Perf 13.
531 45c. Gray, pink, and olive-green 40 15

412. Pierre-Joseph Pelletier and Joseph Bienaime Caventou with Quinine Formula

413. Flamingo

1970, 28 March. **Launch of the rocket *Diamant B* from Guyana.**
Designed and engraved by Combet. Recess. Perf 13
532 45c Blue-green 20 15

1970, 4 April. **World Health Organization Fight Cancer Day.**
Designed and engraved by Decaris. Recess. Perf 13.
533 40c plus 10c. Olive-brown, pink, and blue 20 20

STAMP TERMS

You will come across many unfamiliar terms in stamp books, magazines, and catalogs. Most of the ones that are commonly used by stamp collectors are explained elsewhere in this book: for example, the printing term "intaglio" is explained on page 48, under How Stamps Are Made. If you need to know what a word or phrase means, you can use the index on page 76 to help you find a description of it.

On these two pages you will find some more definitions of the technical terms that are used to describe stamps and other philatelic items, and a diagram showing what the parts of a stamp are called.

Adhesive Postage Stamp. Stamp affixed by gum, as opposed to handstamped, embossed, or printed onto a postal item.

Aerogramme. Lightweight pre-stamped stationery that folds to form its own envelope.

Aniline. A fugitive ink, that is, one that runs when immersed in water.

Backstamp. Postmark applied to a postal item's back.

Bisect. Stamp cut in half and used at half of its original value.

Block. Four or more stamps joined together, but at least two across and two down.

Bogus Stamp. Stamp issued for a fictitious place or postal service or for political propaganda purposes.

Booklet. Small panes of stamps bound together between covers. Modern panes usually have a single pane stuck to a folded cardboard cover.

Cachet. An inscription on a card or cover marking a special event, usually applied by handstamp.

CDS. Abbreviation for "circular datestamp."

Cover. An envelope or wrapper used in the mail.

CTO. Abbreviation for "canceled to order." These are stamps that, though canceled, have not performed a postal service.

Die. An original engraved plate used to prepare a printing plate.

Duplex Cancel. Postmark in which the datestamp and canceling device form one piece.

Embossing. Method of printing where the paper is given a raised effect.

Entire. A complete envelope or other postal item.

Essay. A stamp design that has not been used, or has been used with alterations.

Facsimile. A reproduction of a genuine stamp. A facsimile is usually marked in some way and is not intended to defraud.

FDC. Abbreviation for first-day cover.

Field Post Office. Post office used by troops on maneuvers or active service.

Frank. Stamp or other mark used to show that mail should be carried without charge.

Gutter. The "selvage" (blank space) between panes of a sheet of stamps.

Imprint. Inscription (usually the printer's name) found in the margin of a sheet of stamps or on the stamps themselves.

Jubilee Line. Colored line found in the margins of a sheet of British stamps.

Key Plate. Plate that prints a common design for several countries.

Key Type. Stamp printed in a common design for several countries.

Killer. Cancellation that heavily obliterates a stamp to prevent its reuse.

Miniature Sheet. A small sheet containing one or more stamps, usually without decorative margins.

Mint. Unused stamp as issued.

Mint Set. Issued annually by the U.S. Postal Service, a collection of all the commemoratives issued in one year. Definitive sets are also issued, but less frequently.

Mixed Postage. Cover or card with the stamps of two or more countries.

Mounted Mint. Unused stamp (mint) with hinge marks on the back.

Obsolete. Stamp no longer available from post offices, although possibly still postally valid.

Original Gum. Stamp possessing some of the gum present at the time of issue. Abbreviated to O.G.

Pane. The unit into which a full sheet of stamps is divided before being shipped to post offices. Also a leaf of stamps from a stamp booklet.

Paquebot. French term for Packet Boat. Describes mail sent onboard ship and later taken ashore for onward mailing. Such mail often has a special cancellation.

Perfin. Stamp perforated with initials or other design, usually by a company, to prevent theft.

PHQ Card. A postcard produced by the British Post Office when new stamps are issued, reproducing the stamp designs.

Postal Fiscal. Fiscal stamp used for postage.

Precancel. Stamp bearing a printed cancellation for

STAMP TERMS

PARTS OF A STAMP

This pair of Maltese 4-centime and 25-centime commemorative stamps shows many features commonly found on postage stamps. These two, which have different designs and values, are described as a "se tenant" pair when joined together in this way. When se tenant stamps form a complete picture it is called a composite design.

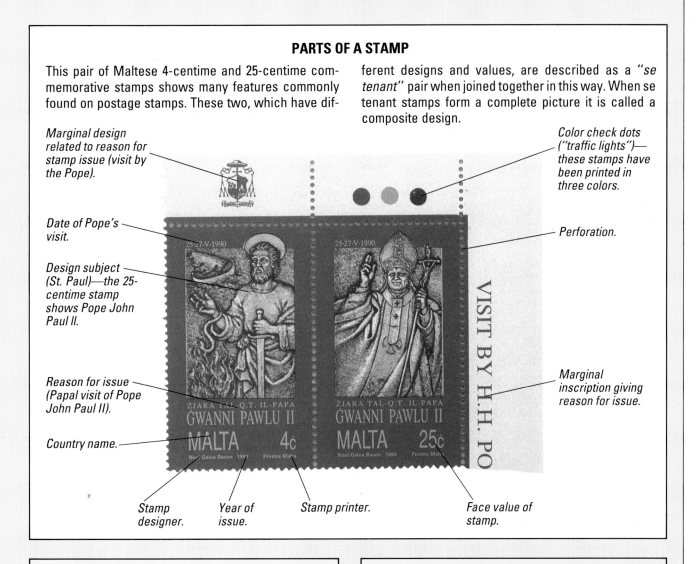

Marginal design related to reason for stamp issue (visit by the Pope).

Color check dots ("traffic lights")—these stamps have been printed in three colors.

Date of Pope's visit.

Perforation.

Design subject (St. Paul)—the 25-centime stamp shows Pope John Paul II.

Reason for issue (Papal visit of Pope John Paul II).

Marginal inscription giving reason for issue.

Country name.

Stamp designer.

Year of issue.

Stamp printer.

Face value of stamp.

use on bulk mailings.

Provisional. Stamp overprinted or surcharged for use during a temporary shortage or other emergency.

Reentry. A doubling of the design on a line-engraved stamp (see page 48). It is caused by a new impression of the design being placed over a partly erased one.

Selvage. The marginal paper on a sheet of stamps.

Space-filler. Substandard stamp used in a collection until a better one is found.

Strip. Three or more stamps joined together in a row.

Tab. An additional piece of paper perforated to the bottom of a stamp.

Traffic Lights. Colored dots found in the gutter of multicolored printed stamps, one dot for each color. They are used to check that all the colors have been printed.

Transit Mark. Postmark applied during an item's journey between point of mailing and point of arrival.

Universal Postal Union (UPU). A body that organizes postal cooperation between different countries. Founded in 1874, it is based in Berne, Switzerland.

Unmounted Mint. A stamp as issued—one that has never been hinged.

Unused. Stamp that has not passed through the mail, but that has a hinge mark or some other mark that keeps it from being mint.

Used. A stamp that has been canceled.

Vignette. The central portion of a stamp, strictly one that shades off at the edges.

Wing Margin. A wide margin on some early letterpress-printed British stamps, where a gutter between stamp panes was perforated through the center instead of near the stamp design.

TYPES OF STAMPS

The first postage stamps were issued as a handy method of paying in advance—prepaying—for the delivery of mail. Printed in sheets, most of them pictured the president, monarch, or emblem of the issuing country. Their basic format is still kept by many countries today, although some have become larger, with pictorial designs. These everyday stamps are known to collectors as definitive, permanent, or regular issues.

It is easy to overlook definitive stamps, which many people think remain the same for years. In fact new values, watermarks, perforations, or other variations appear quite frequently, providing a large number of stamps that can be collected by those who enjoy studying their subtle differences.

CHARITY STAMPS

Charity stamps are issued by many countries. In addition to the normal postage, they carry a small extra charge (usually shown separately on the stamp), which is given to charity. Annual charity stamps have been issued by France, Germany, Switzerland, New Zealand, and the Netherlands for many years.

Charity stamps are a popular way of raising funds for welfare, children's needs, and other worthy causes. Those shown are issued on an annual basis.

Early definitives often pictured a country's president, coat of arms, or monarch. Modern issues (left) feature a wide variety of subjects.

British regional or "country" stamps (above) are issued for Northern Ireland, Scotland, and Wales.

DEFINITIVE DESIGNS

Many countries have issued definitives in the same design for years. Norway's Posthorn design first appeared in 1871, and variations of it were still appearing more than 100 years later. Great Britain's definitives were first issued in 1967. The decimal version was introduced in 1971, when decimal currency (100 pennies = one pound) replaced the Imperial currency (12 pennies = one shilling, 20 shillings = one pound). More than 150 basic variations are now listed in stamp catalogs.

BOOKLETS AND COILS

Stamp booklets and coil stamps (ones printed in long strips) are issued by many countries as convenient ways of buying stamps. Sweden's stamps are sold only in these forms.

Booklets and coil stamps often provide variations of similar stamps issued in sheets. For example, the stamps may have one or more edges that are without perforations, as shown by this example of three U.S. stamps. Also shown are South African and Swedish stamps.

Some postage stamps are sold only in booklet form. These booklets can make a fascinating study in their own right, and many have attractive pictorial covers that can add interest to a topical collection.

COMMEMORATIVE STAMPS

Stamps issued for special occasions probably form the largest group. Most are larger than definitives and depict an enormous number of subjects. The first commemorative stamps issued by a government authority were those of New South Wales (Australia) in 1888 for the centenary of British settlement. Commemoratives issued by a number of countries at the same time to mark the same event are known as "omnibus issues." The first was issued by Portugal and its colonies in 1898. British colonies made many such issues, the first in 1935 for King George V's Silver Jubilee (a British anniversary celebration when a king has reigned for twenty-five years).

The world's first commemorative (above left) and a black-bordered "mourning stamp" (above).

MOUNTING BOOKLETS

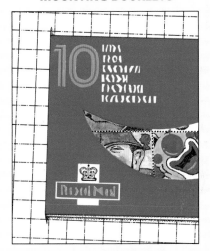

Some stamp booklets are very thick, which makes them difficult to mount with photo corners. Instead, cut two vertical slits, to the height of the booklet and about an inch apart, in the album page. Then slide the booklet's back cover between them.

Greetings stamps (above) have been issued by many countries for use on personal mail.

Commemorative stamps (right) cover a wide range of subjects. How many of these do you recognize?

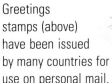

AIRMAIL STAMPS

Definitives and commemoratives are not the only sorts of stamp you will come across. Stamps have been issued for many special purposes. For example, airmail stamps were widely issued during the pioneer years of flight, when airmail routes were being developed; they often commemorated special flights. Today, when airmail is common, few countries issue them. Instead, special airmail stickers and envelopes indicate that an item is to travel by air.

Airmail stamps (above) were very popular in the early years of route development. Many of them are now scarce.

POST-OFFICE SERVICES

Stamps have been issued for several other special services provided by postal authorities including express (next day) delivery, registered mail (for which the addressee must sign a receipt), and delivery of newspapers, printed matter, and parcels. In 1913 Italy issued stamps for mail carried by a pneumatic tube system, a series of underground tubes through which mail was carried by air pressure. Special stamps for use by government departments and by soldiers on active military service have also appeared.

"Postage due" stamps serve another purpose. They are used for collecting money from the addressee on unpaid or underpaid mail. They are also used to collect customs duties on mail sent from abroad. If you find one of these stamps on an envelope, do not remove it. Left on the envelope, it will show that it has performed its service. It will be an interesting addition to your collection.

Special Delivery, Parcel Post, and Express stamps (above and right)

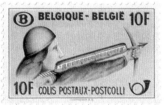

Above left, a War Tax stamp from Bahrain. Left, a Belgian Railway Parcel stamp, and an Italian *Poste Militaire* (Military Post) stamp.

Italian stamps for use on letters carried in pneumatic tubes (left); and a Montserrat (a British island) stamp (right) overprinted for official use ("On Her Majesty's Service").

AUTOMATIC STAMPS

Some unusual stamps look like the "stamp" part of a meter mark (a form of postmark, see page 63). These stamps have been introduced by many countries and are produced by electronic vending machines. After inserting money, the purchaser presses a button to select the value of stamp required; the machine then prints the stamp, often on specially patterned paper. These automatic stamps are sometimes called Framas after the manufacturer of one of the machines that produces them. Another name for them is ATMs, an abbreviation of the German word *Automatenmarken* (automatic stamp).

Two Postage Due stamps (above).

POSTAL STATIONERY

Many authorities issue stationery items other then adhesive postal stamps. These include postcards, aerogrammes, and envelopes with stamps printed on them. In addition to the stamps, postal stationery often has pictorial designs that commemorate a special event or feature the country of issue.

Two postal stationery items inspired by philatelic subjects are, above left, a San Marino postcard and, center, an envelope from Australia. An Austrian aerogramme is shown below.

VALUABLE STAMPS

Of the countless millions of stamps ever issued, there are many that are worth considerable sums of money. This is usually because there are very few of them or because they contain a spectacular error.

EARLY STAMPS

In 1847 the remote Indian Ocean island of Mauritius, then a British colony, issued a postage stamp. Engraved by Joseph Barnard, a watchmaker in the island's capital of Port Louis, these ld (one penny) and 2d (two penny) stamps bear a crude portrait of Queen Victoria. Instead of the words "Post Paid," Barnard engraved "Post Office." Most of these Post Office stamps were used by the governor's wife, Lady Gomm, on invitations to a government ball. Only 500 of each value were printed, and very few now exist.

Bermuda's first stamps (above). Mauritius Post Paid stamps (right) are similar to the rare Post Office version.

Bermuda's first stamps were produced by its postmaster, William Perot, in 1848. He used his postmark canceler to make the stamps, which were sold for a penny each. The stamps were intended for use on letters put in the mailbox after the post office had closed; during open hours, mail was paid for in cash and these stamps were not used. These "Perots" were intended for local use only, and very few have survived.

STAMPS ON STAMPS

Most of us are unlikely to own one of the famous rarities mentioned on these pages. However, we can have them in our albums by forming a collection of "stamps on stamps"—a popular theme. Most of these famous issues, and many others, have appeared on more common stamps. Stamp anniversaries and stamp exhibitions often provide an excuse for depicting them.

A British Guiana "cotton-reel." The stamps were initialed before sale to prevent fraud.

The world's "rarest stamp"—the unique British Guiana one-cent stamp.

This 3-skilling banco stamp from Sweden should be green, not yellow.

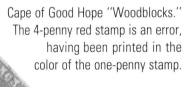

This Western Australia stamp has its frame inverted, though it is popularly known as the "Inverted Swan."

SCHOOLBOY DISCOVERIES

Perhaps the world's most famous stamp, the British Guiana one-cent black on magenta, was discovered by a schoolboy in British Guiana in 1873. The only one of its kind, this stamp has been described as the world's rarest stamp.

Another valuable stamp from British Guiana is the "cottonreel" of 1850, so called because its shape looked like the label at the end of a cottonreel.

One of Europe's rarest stamps is from Sweden. Like the British Guiana stamp, it too was discovered by a schoolboy. This stamp, the 3-skilling banco of 1857, contains an error of color. It is yellow, the color of the 8-skilling banco, instead of green. The error was caused by an incorrect part being put into the printing plate when it was made.

The central figure is missing from this Virgin Island stamp: it is called the "Missing Virgin."

ERRORS

A similar mistake caused the Cape of Good Hope triangular "Woodblocks" to be printed in the wrong colors. The one-penny was in blue instead of red, and the 4-penny in red instead of blue. (These locally produced stamps were called "Woodblocks" because they looked as if they had been printed from wood engravings.) Other famous errors include the "Missing Virgin" on the 1867 Virgin Islands one-shilling stamp, the Western Australia "Inverted Swan" of 1854 (actually an inverted frame), and the inverted Curtiss "Jenny" airplane on a 1918 U.S. airmail stamp.

Cape of Good Hope "Woodblocks." The 4-penny red stamp is an error, having been printed in the color of the one-penny stamp.

UNUSUAL STAMPS

Most of us think of stamps as being small, rectangular pieces of paper, usually perforated, with a design on one side and gum on the other. This is usually so, but there are many strange exceptions.

SHAPES
The first non-rectangular stamp design, an octagonal one, was issued by Great Britain in 1847—though the stamps were often cut square from the unperforated sheet. A triangular stamp appeared from the Cape of Good Hope in 1853, and there have been many since. Other shapes have also been used, from diamond to circular. Perhaps the strangest are the "free-forms" of Sierra Leone and Tonga. These are in exotic shapes, such as parrots, bananas, watermelons, athletes, and maps. Norfolk Island, in the South Pacific, has also issued map-shaped stamps. Many of these were self-adhesive. Another unusual stamp was produced by Gibraltar in 1969, perforated to the shape of the famous Rock of Gibraltar.

Stamps have been printed and embossed on gold foil (below left). The backs of maps and bank notes have been used for Latvian stamps (below right).

This map-shaped Sierra Leone stamp (left) is on self-adhesive paper, as are the two rectangular ones below.

Strange shapes include some of the many triangular stamps produced. The Colombian stamp (top left) is one of the smallest.

Left, a miniature sheet from Paraguay with a record attached. Below is one of a set of stamps from Bhutan that plays folk songs and the national anthem.

PRINTING MATERIALS

Paper is the most common printing surface for a stamp, and lots of different kinds of paper have been used. Many other materials, such as cloth, metal foils, steel, plastic, and wood veneer, have been used as well. Stamps have also been printed on the backs of old bank notes and maps.

The Himalayan country of Bhutan has issued many unusual stamps, including scented and plastic-molded ones, and, strangest of all, gramophone-record stamps that play the country's national anthem. Paraguay, too, has issued a philatelic gramophone record, which was stuck to a miniature sheet depicting the band Los Paraguayos.

JOINED AND INVERTED

Stamps of two or more different designs joined together have been issued by many countries. Stamps joined in this way are known as *se tenant*, from the French for "joined together." Where the different designs form one picture it is called a composite design.

When one stamp is upside down in relation to another, the stamps are said to be *tête-bêche* (which, loosely translated from the French, means "top against bottom"). Such stamps are usually issued in error.

Se tenant stamps. Those from Kiribati have a composite design.

A block of Swiss stamps printed tête-bêche.

THREE DIMENSIONS

The first stamp with a 3-D (three-dimensional) image came from Italy in 1956 to commemorate the United Nations. It depicted a map of the world which, when viewed through special glasses with red and green lenses, appeared to be three-dimensional. Bhutan has also issued a stamp printed on a special kind of plastic that gives a 3-D appearance. In 1988, Austria issued a stamp incorporating a hologram (which gives a 3-D image), and the U.S. has produced postal stationery envelopes incorporating holograms.

Special glasses are needed to see the 3-D effect of the Italian stamp above. Holograms (right) require no special aids.

COLLECTING BY COUNTRY

Most collectors probably begin by collecting the stamps of the world. Sooner or later, however, they find that there are far too many stamps for this to be worthwhile, and they begin limiting their collections. The traditional way of doing this is to collect the stamps of just one or two countries. This still makes for plenty to collect.

CHOOSING A COUNTRY

Which country should you choose? Most people find that collecting the stamps of the country where they live makes the most sense. First of all, it is usually easy to obtain information about one's native stamps. Also, new issues can be purchased directly from a post office, older stamps are quite likely to be found at a stamp dealer's, and swapping with fellow collectors should be easy.

You might choose other countries because you already have a lot of stamps from them, or because you have friends or relatives in a foreign country who can keep you supplied with stamps. Or maybe you find a particular country's stamps attractive because of their designs or the way they are printed.

GREAT BRITAIN
April 25, 1975
European Architectural Heritage Year

June 11, 1975
Sailing

UNITED STATES
Great Americans

CANCELLATIONS

Stamps may be collected used or unused; but they should always be in good condition. Do not include damaged or heavily postmarked stamps in your collection, because they will spoil its appearance. However, used stamps with suitable postmarks are often quite difficult to find. Shown here are some used stamps that have different grades of cancellation.

A neat date stamp (top left). Light slogan cancels (top right) are OK, but avoid heavy ones (right).

The Christmas slogan (above) and postmark (right) obscure the design.

Pages from straightforward British and U.S. collections (left). Their blank pages allow for flexibility in the layout. The Australian collection below is mounted on pre-printed pages, which allows less room for expansion.

AUSTRALIA

2 — 16th October. Tenth International Congress of Account-, Sydney. Designed by G. Andrews; printed by the Reserve of Australia. No watermark.
13 x 13½.

2 — 15th November. Pioneer Life. Designed by R. Ingpen; ted by the Reserve Bank of Australia. No watermark.
13½ x 13 (5c, 10c, 60c), 13 x 13½ (others).

72 — 29th November. Christmas. Designs adapted by W. Tamlyn) and L. Stirling (35c); printed by the Reserve Bank of Australia. watermark.
f 13 x 13½.

LOOKING AHEAD

Before you begin to collect a country's stamps seriously, it is a good idea to see what is involved by taking a look through a stamp catalog. Many countries have issued so many stamps that it would be nearly impossible to obtain them all; another country's stamps might be so expensive that you could never afford them. For example, Great Britain has issued more than 1,500 stamps in total, including 70 in 1991; France 3,000 (60 in 1991); the U.S. 2,500 (70 in 1991) and Germany (West and Berlin) about 2,000 (90 in 1991). In such cases it might be a good idea to limit the scope of your collection. You could collect stamps of a particular monarch's reign or from a particular period—German stamps since reunification, or those of a country since its independence, for example. You could even collect the stamps of a single issue: there are many sets that lend themselves to this. Long-running definitive sets in particular give plenty of room for study. The different printings, varieties, booklet panes, and other items could form a highly specialized collection.

Choosing a less popular country or one that no longer issues stamps may seem to be a good idea. But it could be difficult to obtain enough stamps to keep you interested in such a collection.

COLLECTOR'S HINT
It is best not to mix used and unused stamps in the same set. Instead, display them as separate sets, either on the same page, below one another, or on a new sheet.

DEVELOPING THE COLLECTION

Just as some countries issue too many stamps to collect, others may not issue enough to keep you busy for long. Instead of starting another collection, you might develop your existing collection by extending it beyond the scope of the catalog. This can involve carefully studying your stamps to find varieties and errors, the addition of stamp booklets and postal stationery or, perhaps, Cinderellas (see page 66).

POSTAL HISTORY

The collection could also be extended backward to show the history of your chosen country's postal service. This could include letters carried before stamps were introduced. Stamps on cover could be collected to show some special use, such as registration or airmail, or they could simply demonstrate the various postal rates that apply to the different weights of mail.

Today, much mail is sorted by machine. Often the envelopes bear markings that show this. Also, many modern postal services do not use stamps at all. Look at the envelopes of business mail and "junk" mail, for example. Such material is often thrown away, yet it is nevertheless part of a country's postal history. A few pages of such material could expand the interest and scope of your collection.

POSTMARKS

Postmarks provide another means of extending your collection. They may reveal that a letter has been sorted on a railroad traveling post office or sent from a ship at sea. If you collect the stamps of a small country, it might be possible to obtain postmarks from every post office. With imagination and study, a substantial small-country collection can be developed. If a larger country is your subject, a range of the postmarks used there may be of interest.

Covers can reveal many aspects of postal services. Shown top to bottom are a British cover sent without a stamp and with postage due markings and label; an underpaid cover sent from the United States with U.S. and British markings; a Belgian Express letter; and a British triangular postmark usually used on mail containing advertising leaflets.

1955-58
DEFINITIVE ISSUE

Watermark St. Edward's Crown.
Watermark sideways ex coils
Varieties

white flaw
over "O"
Coil 2

dot between rose
& thistle at right
Coil 10

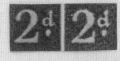

retouched "2" leaving "d"
nearer to "2" and fatter
Coil T(5)

extra leg to "R"
of "REVENUE"
Coil T(2)

A page from a specialized collection of British definitives. The enlarged illustrations point out constant flaws found on the stamps included in the album. The stamps are mounted in protective strips.

COLLECTOR'S HINT
Covers and stationery items can often be overlapped to display only the relevant parts, thus taking up less space in the album.

COLLECTING BY TOPIC

Topical collecting (which is also known as thematic collecting) is an increasingly popular way of forming a stamp collection. Unlike traditional collecting, where the object is to obtain all the stamps of a particular country or period, topical collecting involves choosing stamps by what they depict. A topical collection is likely to contain both old and new stamps from many different countries, and it doesn't have to contain every stamp that has ever been issued on the chosen topic in order to be "complete." Thus, a really interesting and unusual collection can be made inexpensively.

Above are four stamps showing storybook characters —just one of the many hundreds of topics you can choose to collect.

CHOOSING A TOPIC

The choice of topic is huge. Stamps have been issued for just about every subject imaginable. Some topics have large numbers of stamps devoted to them and are extremely popular—birds (over 7,500 stamps), mammals (5,000), ships (11,000), and railroads (6,000) for example. You can also collect by topic on a small scale—a more manageable topic might be mushrooms, of which there are 650 stamps worldwide. Perhaps small topics could provide for a sideline or "fun" collection in addition to your main collection.

Wildlife subjects are very popular. There are thousands of bird stamps (above), but fewer of subjects such as reptiles.

Another popular topic offering room for development is railroads. About 6,000 stamps depicting locomotives and related subjects have been issued.

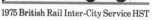

1975 British Rail Inter-City Service HST

A PARTICULAR INTEREST

You will obviously choose your subject because it has some interest to you. Perhaps you enjoy sports or animals. Although you will probably begin by trying to collect all the sports or animal stamps that you can, you will soon find that such a task is too great. You may find that it makes sense to break your subject down further. Try collecting stamps showing a particular sport, such as baseball, soccer, or tennis, or stamps depicting an animal species. The choice is endless. You will probably find that collecting in this way is very interesting.

In many ways, collecting by topic is much more challenging than collecting by country. You will need to search through stamp catalogs to see which stamps fit your topic. And you will need to find out about the subject you have chosen in order to have interesting information accompanying the stamps once they are mounted in your album.

A page from a collection on the topic of cats. Simple captions explain the stamps. There are many catalogs and checklists available to help you build topical collections.

COLLECTOR'S HINT
Always remember that a topical collection is a stamp collection. Be very sparing in the use of items other than philatelic ones, such as photographs.

Charles Dickens was born in Portsmouth, England, on February 7, 1812. His early life was spent in hardship, experiences reflected in DAVID COPPERFIELD. He began his writing career as a reporter. Most of his novels were originally published in serial form. In 1853 he began charity readings of his works. A tour to the United States in 1867 undermined his failing health and he died, aged 58, on June 9, 1870 at Gads Hill, Kent, England. He wrote 16 novels.

SCENES FROM THE NOVELS

SOCCER

A STORY IN STAMPS

Topical stamp collecting can be as simple as just obtaining stamps showing a certain subject. It can be more challenging, too, if the stamps are used to illustrate the development of a story or an idea. For example, instead of forming a haphazard collection of stamps issued for the Olympic Games, the history and growth of the Olympic Games could be told through the stamps. Such a collection might begin with the Games' origins in ancient Greece, show their development, the ceremonies that took place, the buildings at the Olympic site, as well as the various sports that were contested. It might then move on to the modern Games and show why they were reintroduced, their gradual development, the cities that have hosted them, the people who helped organize them, famous athletes, the introduction of the Winter Games, and so on. In order to tell its story well, a collection like this would probably contain many postal items that were not issued to commemorate the Games themselves.

There are two major types of
elephant : African and Indian.

Elephants can be seen on safari. In the East, elephants are
used as working animals and on ceremonial occasions.

Elephants can be seen in
zoos and at the circus.

FIRST DAY COVER

"RAJA" TUSKER OF SRI DALADA MALIGAWA

Shown are pages
from three topical
collections. Note the
different styles and
amounts of
information included
on the pages. A
stamp booklet and
first-day cover have
been used in the
elephant collection.

CAREFUL RESEARCH

In order to develop a story or idea through stamps,
you will need to research your subject well. Once you
understand the subject, you will be able to see how
seemingly unrelated stamps will fit into the collection. You will need to write some notes that link your
stamps together on the album page and develop the
story you are telling. This will help other people
make sense of your collection. Such a collection may
be difficult to form, but it will also be very rewarding.

PLANNING

To form any topical collection, you need to have a
plan in mind. A collection of animal stamps could
simply be divided into types of animals from aard-
vark to zebra. One on horses would need more
careful thought. For example, it might show the
different breeds and their uses in farming, transport,
and sports. Write out a brief plan showing the way
you intend to develop your topic. This will help you
see how and where a particular stamp will fit in.

VARIATIONS ON A THEME

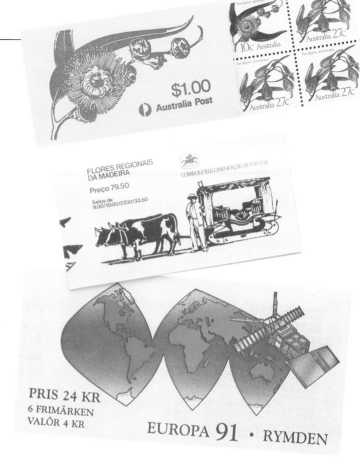

A topical collection need not be devoted only to stamps. The addition of other philatelic material that helps to tell your story, such as postmarks and postal stationery, can give your collection much more variety.

POSTMARKS

Stamps in a topical collection are generally best collected unused so that the designs are clear. However, postmarks play an important part in their own right. There are many pictorial postmarks that will fit into a topic. These may depict a related subject—a person or building, for example—or may commemorate an event that fits into your story. Meter marks (see page 63) and postmarks with advertising slogans on them can fit in, too. If they also cancel a stamp that is part of the theme, so much the better. Postmarks should be clear and easily read.

Below are special-event and slogan postmarks useful for a ships collection (left), and two air-related meter marks.

These stamp-booklet covers will fit topical collections of flowers, animals, transport, space, and maps.

George J. King,
42, Arundel Road,
Kingston, Surrey.

DISPLAYING POSTMARKS

If the complete envelope is not needed, then the postmark and stamp can be cut out neatly and mounted on the page. On the other hand, you might want to keep the envelope complete, but do not want to take up too much room on the album page. To do this, cut a rectangular hole in the page and mount the envelope behind it. The stamp and the postmark will show through the hole.

STATIONERY

Postal stationery items—postcards, envelopes, and aerogrammes—are issued by many countries. The printed stamps on these items often have a suitable design that will fit a topical collection, and many also have other pictorial elements that can be useful. Australia often issues pre-stamped envelopes to commemorate subjects not thought important enough for a stamp. The U.S. and Italy also issue many pictorial stationery items, and aerogrammes are produced by countries throughout the world. Stamp booklets often have pictorial covers, and so should not be overlooked. "Cinderella" items (explained on page 66) can also be included.

STAMP DETAILS

Take a close look at your stamps, because just a tiny part of a design will often be found to fit a topic. Look out, too, for watermarks. These often overlooked parts of a stamp can provide some surprises: some stamps from Tonga, for example, have a tortoise watermark that perhaps could fit an animal collection.

Overprints can be a source of designs, and labels found attached to some stamps may also be useful. Varieties and errors can add interest to any collection—a topical one is no exception.

Flower overprint

Tongan tortoise watermark

Advertisement attached to Italian stamp

EUROFLORA '81 GENOVA
25 APRILE - 3 MAGGIO

PAR AVION

1838-1988 150th Anniversary
South Australian Police

37c Australia

Items of postal stationery—pre-stamped aerogrammes (above), envelopes (center), and postcards (right)—often have interesting and colorful designs that will fit into a topical collection.

HOW STAMPS ARE MADE

The process from an original idea to a finished stamp is complex. From the hundreds of suggestions for stamp issues made each year—by individuals, or organizations wanting to commemorate an event—postal administrations have to select just a few to make interesting issuing programs. It can take two or three years before a stamp is finally put on sale.

THE ARTIST

Having decided on a stamp issue, a postal administration asks one or more artists to produce suitable designs. The artists set to work, researching the subject to make sure the design is correct. When the research is complete, artwork, in the form of a drawing, painting, or photograph, is presented for consideration by the postal administration. This presentation includes the proposed lettering and other design elements. Once a design has been selected, any alterations that are needed are carried out. The finished artwork is usually prepared in a much larger size than the printed stamp. Once the postal administration has approved it, the artwork is sent to the printer.

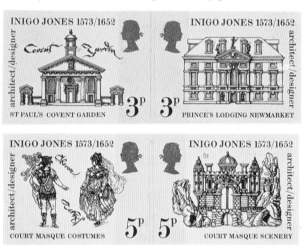

PERFORATION AND ROULETTE

The first stamps were cut from the printed sheet with scissors. The use of perforated sheets, which have rows of tiny holes punched between the stamps, makes it easier to separate them neatly.

Sheets that are perforated row by row, first in one direction and then the other, are described as "line perforated." Stamps perforated in this way often have corners that are uneven, because the perforation holes do not coincide. This unevenness is particularly noticeable on blocks of stamps.

A "comb perforator"—so called because it looks like a comb—perforates the top and sides of a stamp in one operation. It moves down the sheet, one row of stamps at a time, in one direction only. The holes where the lines cross over at the corners of the stamps are usually even and regular.

AT THE PRINTER

What happens next depends on the printing process used. If the stamp is to be printed by the intaglio method, a skilled engraver engraves the design, in reverse, onto a block of metal. During his work, proofs, or test printings, are taken to check its progress.

The finished die, or engraved plate, will be hardened and the image transferred, under pressure, to a transfer roller; the design now appears the right way around. This roller is in turn hardened and used to place the design, again in reverse, on the printing plate, once for each stamp in the sheet. Color proofs may be taken from the die in order to make sure that the colors are printing properly.

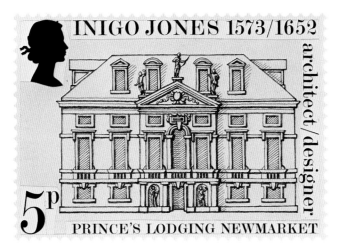

PHOTOCHEMICAL PROCESSES

When a stamp is printed either by the photogravure or litho method (see pages 48 and 49), a photochemical process is used to transfer the stamp design the required number of times to a printing cylinder or plate. If the stamp is to be printed in more than one color, a separate plate is needed for each. When the printing plates are put onto a printing press, proofs are made. These proofs are checked and, if necessary, the colors are adjusted. Once the presses are correctly adjusted, the stamps are produced.

Most multicolored stamps are printed from just four colors: yellow, cyan (blue), magenta (red), and black. However, most multicolored stamps printed by the photogravure method (see next page) use many more different-colored inks to achieve their effect. By using a magnifying glass you can see the tiny dots of ink that make up the stamp's picture.

Stamp-size essays, or designs (far left); the original artwork; the final redrawn artwork before the colors, values, and pairings have been finalized; and, above, the issued stamps.

PRINTING

Stamps may be printed in sheets or in a continuous roll that is cut into single sheets. The sheets are perforated either as part of the printing process or in a separate operation. The finished sheets are checked for errors, counted, and finally distributed to post offices for use.

Another means of separating stamps is called "rouletting." The paper is cut or pierced but, unlike perforation, no paper is removed. There are many types of roulette pattern—arc, cross, diamond, lozenge, pin, sawtooth, serpentine, and zigzag are names for some of them.

PRINTING STAMPS

There are four main methods of printing stamps. Sometimes two of these, usually intaglio and either photogravure or lithography, are combined in one stamp. This allows for an engraved design (which collectors consider the best method for printing stamps, but which cannot be used to produce a multicolored design) in full color.

INTAGLIO

This printing method, also known to philatelists as line engraving or recess printing, was used to print the Penny Black. The design is cut into the printing surface, which is then inked and wiped, leaving the ink in the cut lines. Paper laid on the printing surface, under pressure, then picks up the ink of the design. The printed design can usually be felt as a slightly raised surface.

PHOTOGRAVURE

A modern variation of intaglio is photogravure. With this method, a photographic negative of the stamp design is broken into a screen of small dots and etched onto a copper cylinder. Each dot of the design forms a tiny cell in the cylinder and varies in depth. When printing, the cylinder is inked and wiped, leaving ink in the cells: the shallow cells hold less ink, giving a light tone; the deeper cells hold more, giving a darker tone. Look through a magnifying glass to see the tiny dots that form a photogravure stamp's design. The dots are particularly noticeable along the edges of letters and numbers, which appear ragged.

OTHER PRINTING METHODS

Photography has rarely been used to print stamps, though it is used in the production process to make printing plates. The most famous photographically printed stamps are those made during the Boer War's Siege of Mafeking (South Africa) in 1900. The 3-penny value depicts Colonel Baden-Powell, the founder of the Boy Scouts.

Stamps have also been produced using a typewriter—this one is from Long Island. Typewriters have also been used to over-print and surcharge stamps.

LETTERPRESS

Also called surface printing or typography, letterpress is the opposite of intaglio. The design is engraved, but the areas *not* required to print do not touch the printing surface.
Ink is applied to the raised surface of the design, which is transferred to the paper. Stamps printed directly from printers' metal type are printed by this method. The pressure applied when printing sometimes leaves a slightly raised impression of the design on the back of the stamp, and the ink can squeeze somewhat over the edges of the design. This, too, can be seen with a magnifying glass.

LITHOGRAPHY

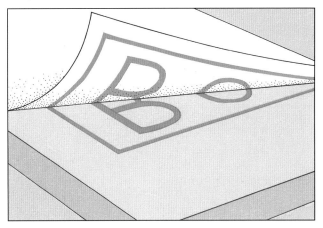

Common in modern stamp printing, lithography uses the fact that oil and water do not mix. A special greasy ink is used to transfer the stamp design to a printing surface. The surface is moistened and ink is applied. The ink sticks to the greasy portion of the printing surface, which is then impressed onto the paper. In a variation of this method known as offset litho, the inked image is first impressed onto a rubber "blanket" which prints ("offsets") it onto the paper. Like photogravure stamps, many litho stamps have a "screen" of dots. However, with lithography they are clearer, and lettering viewed under a magnifying glass will be seen to have neat edges.

FORGERIES AND FAKES

Many stamps are worth considerable amounts of money. It is not surprising, therefore, to find that a large number have been forged or tampered with in an attempt to deceive and defraud collectors. Sometimes, attempts are even made to forge a genuine stamp's overprint or postmark.

The Star of David on the crown, and the hammer and sickle forming the *1D*, reveal this German propaganda forgery (above left). The Jersey occupation stamps (right) are not forgeries, but can you spot the *GR* and *V* (for Victory) in the scrolling?

FAMOUS FORGERS

Two famous forgers were Francois Fournier and Jean de Sperati. Fournier, active at the turn of the century, offered his forgeries, which he regarded as works of art, to collectors unable to afford the originals. Sperati produced his work between the two world wars, forging more than 500 different valuable stamps. Today, reference collections of both men's work exist, enabling experts to identify items forged by them.

In the 1870s a forged British one-shilling stamp was used on telegraph forms at the London Stock Exchange (left). Many years later the forgery was discovered by a stamp dealer who noticed that on some stamps the corner check letters had combinations not used on genuine stamps (shown at bottom). The culprit was never caught.

Jean de Sperati, the forger of many valuable stamps

DEFRAUDING THE AUTHORITIES

Not all forgeries are intended to deceive collectors. Many are meant to defraud the postal authorities. They have also been produced by enemy countries during a war. For example, German propaganda forgeries made during World War II based their designs on current British stamps, but with subtle alterations intended to discredit Great Britain.

Forgery still continues today, usually to defraud postal authorities. For example, in April 1991, the *Times* of India reported that five men, three of them postal staff, had been arrested for preparing and selling forged aerogrammes, resulting in a huge loss to the Indian post office.

SECURITY MEASURES

Stamp-issuing authorities often make great efforts to prevent stamps from being forged. An engraved and easily recognizable portrait of Queen Victoria was used for Great Britain's Penny Black because it was considered difficult to forge. The machine-engraved background made the design even more complex.

A watermark is another important security device. Also, fluorescent security markings, visible only in ultraviolet light, have been used on stamps from the Cook Islands, Ecuador, and Hong Kong.

The removal of postmarks is another security problem. To try to prevent this, fugitive inks (which run when immersed in water) and varnish coatings have been used.

The colored-bar security device at the bottom of this stamp makes it hard to copy.

Attempts have been made to remove the pen cancellation from this Australian stamp in order to sell it for more than its real worth.

A copy with false postmark (left) of the valuable 1857 6d stamp from Western Australia.

Forged Irish £1 (one-pound) stamps were used to defraud the Post Office. The forged stamp (top) has line perforations (see page 46), the genuine stamp (bottom) is comb perforated.

FAKES AND FACSIMILES

Genuine stamps that have been altered in some way are known as fakes. A used stamp may have the postmark removed and be re-gummed to make it appear unused. Colors may be changed or perforations added or removed. Damaged stamps that have been repaired are also considered fakes.

Facsimiles, or reproductions, are stamps that have been copied from originals but don't claim to be originals. They are often marked in some way to make it clear that they are not real stamps. Collectors sometimes buy them because they can't afford the real stamps.

The vertical lines between *Postes* and the central oval give away these Suez Canal company forgeries (right): on the genuine stamps they are cross-hatched.

This Gibraltar stamp appears to be a forgery, yet it is not. Its crude perforation is misleading, and only resulted from its being cut from postal stationery.

Copies of two rare stamps (right)—the 1d Post Office Mauritius and the 2c rose cottonreel of British Guiana.

EXPERT COMMITTEES

Detecting forgeries and fakes can be difficult. To help collectors, many large philatelic societies and some dealers offer an "expertizing" service. For a fee, they will examine an item and assess how genuine they believe it to be. This assessment is recorded on a certificate, which can be kept with the stamp.

MISTAKES

Two stamps with inverted centers (above and right).

A color is missing from this se tenant block of bird stamps (below).

Stamps that contain errors made during the printing process are very popular with collectors. Many with missing colors or inverted centers, for example, are quite striking and much sought after. These, and other major errors, such as incorrectly perforated stamps and those printed in the wrong color or on the wrong paper, are often of great value.

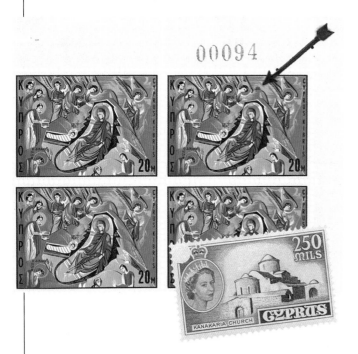

00094

The stamp on the left (see arrow) has a constant flaw. And something on the printing surface has caused the missing corner on the bottom stamp.

This mirror image (above right) has been caused by stacking sheets of stamps that are still wet from printing.

PRINTING FLAWS

There are many minor flaws that can be found on stamps. While not making the stamp very valuable, they add variety to any collection. For example, damage caused to the printing surface at some stage during manufacturing is often so small that it goes unnoticed by the printer. Sharp-eyed collectors soon spot these flaws, however!

Sometimes, after the stamps have been printed and issued, the printer attempts to correct a flaw.

Subsequent printings will show the flaw retouched (corrected). But since this is very hard to do, the correction can often be seen. This provides the collector with yet another item of interest.

When a flaw occurs on every sheet of stamps printed from a plate, it is said to be "constant." Flaws that last for only part of the printing run, perhaps because something sticks to the printing surface and is later removed, are called "inconstant."

The perforations are missing between the two stamps above. Imperforate errors should be collected in pairs.

A flaw on these Hungarian stamps (right) has given one of them a face value of 1.78.

DESIGN ERRORS

Another type of mistake that can be found on stamps is that made in the art. This could be a simple spelling error, an incorrect inscription, or something wrong in the stamp's design. For example, stamps issued by St. Kitts (an island state in the West Indies) in 1903 showed Columbus looking through a telescope, which had not yet been invented in Columbus's time. Sometimes, after such a mistake has been spotted, the stamp is corrected and reissued.

A design error: the airplane on the left has no tail fin—it would be unlikely to fly!

Columbus using a telescope before it was invented!

Above, the French philosopher Descartes and his work *Discours de la Méthode*; the stamp on the right is incorrectly inscribed "Discours sur la Méthode." Left, Governor Phillips meets the "Home Society." The design was also issued with the correct "Home Secretary" caption.

NORFOLK ISLAND

NORFOLK ISLAND

COLLECTOR'S HINT
A small drawing showing an enlarged detail of the stamp, or a paper arrow (stuck to the album page, not the stamp), can help point out difficult-to-see flaws.

EARLY POSTAL SYSTEMS

Although the world's first adhesive postage stamp, the Penny Black, came into use a little over 150 years ago, postal services had been in existence for many hundreds of years before then. There are references to postal services in the Bible. And dating from even earlier (around 3000-2000 BC) are letters on baked clay tablets that have been found in Cappadocia (in modern-day Turkey). These letters even had their own clay envelopes!

A clay letter written in about 2000 BC. The letter still has its protective envelope.

A MESSAGE RELAYED

Messenger services were needed by most ancient civilizations, and were usually organized by the king or by merchants. The first relay postal system is thought to have been founded by King Cyrus, ruler of the Persian Empire, in 539 BC. Stables were set up a day's journey apart, and riders traveling by day and night carried messages between the stables in relays, or rounds. In the Roman Empire, the building of an excellent road network and the well-organized government messenger service, the *Cursus Publicus*, were essential to the smooth functioning of the Empire. The *Cursus Publicus* used both horses and horse-drawn coaches for transport.

Little is known of postal services in Europe after the fall of the Roman Empire, but by the Middle Ages, many different systems existed. They were run by merchants, universities, monasteries, kings and princes, and large towns and cities. The late Middle Ages saw the rise of an international service run by the Thurn and Taxis family of Bavaria. It eventually covered most of Europe and lasted until 1867.

The world's first adhesive postage stamp, the Penny Black (above), was issued by Great Britain in 1840. It depicted a young Queen Victoria.

A stone relief carving of a postal carriage of the *Cursus Publicus*, which carried mail throughout the Roman Empire.

THE FIRST MODERN SYSTEM

In England, Sir Brian Tuke was appointed first Master of the Postes in 1516. Private mail services were discouraged, and after 1591 all mail had to be carried by the royal postal system. The British postal system was well organized but expensive. In the 1830s a retired schoolteacher named Rowland Hill began working for reforms. By 1839, letters were charged by weight rather than by distance traveled. This lowered the cost of postage. In 1840, the introduction of the Penny Black and pre-stamped envelopes made pre-payment of postage much easier.

DEVELOPMENT OF THE U.S. POSTAL SYSTEM

In 1775, the year the Revolutionary War began, the Continental Congress named Benjamin Franklin the first postmaster general of the U.S. In 1783 the nation won its independence, and in 1789 Congress granted the federal government the sole power to provide postal services. That same year, Samuel Osgood was appointed the first postmaster general under the new Constitution of the United States. Postal services expanded rapidly from the 1880s to the early 1900s.

Special postal stationery was issued at the same time as the Penny Black, to pre-pay postage. The design, by William Mulready, was ridiculed by the public and soon withdrawn.

FROM CLAY TO MAILCOACH

Many aspects of early postal systems, from clay tablets to mailcoaches, have been illustrated on stamps. They can make an interesting collection about postal history.

A Cappadocian stone tablet.

A Roman mail cart used in Gaul (France).

A Roman courier on horseback.

The Counts of Thurn and Taxis (above) ran an international service.

A 14th-16th century Russian messenger.

A German messenger from Nuremberg, about 1700.

An Irish mailcoach with outside passengers.

AIRMAIL

Although the first successful airplane—the Wright Brothers' *Flyer*—took to the skies in 1903, mail had been carried by air long before then. In fact, pigeons were the first means of carrying mail by air. They were used by the Romans to carry messages.

The German zeppelins (above and left) introduced regular airmail services. The cover (below) was carried on an airplane launched by catapult in the mid-Atlantic from the French ship *Isle de France* (see page 59).

PIGEONS AND BALLOONS

Pigeons were later used during the Franco-Prussian War (1870-71), when Paris was surrounded by the German army. Photographically reduced messages were flown into the city by pigeons that had been smuggled out by balloon. The balloons, too, were used to fly mail out of the city. But because they could not be steered, they could fly only when weather permitted. Items flown from Paris in this way are much sought after.

Later, motor-powered "dirigible," or steerable, balloons were built. The most famous of these were the German zeppelins, which made possible the regular carriage of mail by balloon. From the late 1920s, zeppelins made many well-publicized flights around the world. Mail carried on these flights often bears colorful handstamps detailing the journey.

A copy of the journal *Gazette des Absents,* flown from Paris by balloon during the siege of 1870-71.

AIRPLANES

Meanwhile, the first airplanes had begun to carry mail. During these early years, mail was often carried to aviation meetings for publicity purposes and as a souvenir of the event. Of course, as the airplane developed, so did airmail routes. Mail was often flown on pioneering flights, and special stamps were sometimes provided for the journeys. For example, Newfoundland issued several stamps for early transatlantic flights.

A card from the world's first official airmail flight (top); a Newfoundland airmail cover (right); an overprint for the first transatlantic airmail in 1919 (far right); an Italian aerogramme depicting the 50th anniversary of a 1940 transatlantic flight (below); and a modern first-flight cover (bottom).

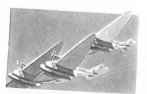

The world's first official airmail was carried between Allahabad and Naini, India, in February 1911. The U.S., Great Britain, Denmark, and Italy all followed with flights in September of the same year. The world's first continuous regular airmail service started in 1918, with U.S. Army pilots flying between New York City, Philadelphia, and Washington, D.C.

In these first years, airmail services could not be taken for granted: worldwide, many pilots were killed while flying their low-performance aircraft. Nevertheless, the demand for quick and regular air communications helped to speed up the development of better and more reliable aircraft.

AIRMAIL TODAY

New airmail services are still being introduced today. Usually, the first flight on a new airmail route is commemorated by a souvenir cover, and often by a special postmark, as well. These first-flight covers can be used in a collection to show the development of airmail routes around the world.

UNUSUAL POSTAL SERVICES

Most of us take for granted the ease with which we can buy a stamp and put our mail into a box for delivery by the postman on his daily round. Yet in many remote and inaccessible places it is not so easy to receive and send mail.

BY LAND...

Most forms of transport—from foot to modern sophisticated vehicle—have been used to carry mail by land. Animals have even been used in some areas. For example, between 1846 and 1904 a service using bullock-drawn carts operated in India. Reindeer have drawn mail sleighs over the difficult terrain of Scandinavia and Russia. Dogs have been used in England and Alaska, and cats in Belgium! And camels have been employed not only in Africa and the Middle East, where you might expect to see them, but also in Australia and the U.S. during the 19th century.

Letters sealed in zinc containers were floated down the River Seine during the Franco-Prussian War's Siege of Paris (right).

Throwing letters in bottles into the sea (left) does not guarantee delivery!

This Botswana stamp (above) depicts the carrying of mail in Africa by the Mafeking to Gubulaway Runner Post.

Carrying mail by foot. This Maori (New Zealand) postman (above) is carrying the mail in a plaited bag.

Mail in India was transported by bullock-drawn carts (left). The famous Pony Express (below) carried mail across the rugged country of the western U.S.

A 17th-century hand-drawn sled and a later horse-drawn sleigh were used to convey mail over Russia's icy wastes (above left). In contrast, camels have carried mail across the world's deserts.

WATER...

War can prevent mail from being delivered. When Paris was besieged by the Germans in 1870-71 (see page 56), not only was mail flown out of the city by balloon, but some mail came into the city in water-tight zinc balls (*boules de Moulins*) that had been sent down the River Seine!

Equally resourceful were the inhabitants of the remote Scottish island of St. Kilda. They sealed letters in hollowed-out driftwood attached to an inflated sheep's bladder. These packages were cast adrift in the North Atlantic, where current and wind, with luck, carried them to shore on the mainland. This mail system was still in use when the island was evacuated in 1930.

Similarly, mail from the Pacific island of Niuafo'ou, Tonga, was at one time sealed in a tin box and rowed out to the waiting mail ship. Colorful Tin Can Mail markings can be found on letters carried by this unusual system.

Mail from the Pacific island of Niuafo'ou (left and below) was sealed in tin cans and taken out to mail ships.

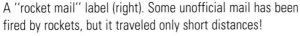

... AND AIR

Carrying mail by air is probably the fastest and most direct method. Just about every form of flight has been used, from pigeon to jet. At first, flying mail long distances over water was fraught with danger.

In the 1920s and 1930s, therefore, experiments were made to catapult, or launch, mail-carrying aircraft from ships in the mid-Atlantic, thus speeding delivery. The first successful flight was made from the French ship *Isle de France* in 1928. Later, the small seaplane *Mercury* was carried into the air by the larger *Maia*. The faster *Mercury* was then launched from *Maia* to deliver the mail more quickly!

Carried piggyback fashion, the mail-carrying *Mercury* (left) was launched from a larger flying-boat in midair.

Catapult-launched airplanes were used to shorten delivery times across the Atlantic. Here (above) a plane is launched from the German ship *Westfalen*.

A "rocket mail" label (right). Some unofficial mail has been fired by rockets, but it traveled only short distances!

FIRST-DAY COVERS

A first-day cover is an envelope bearing a stamp postmarked on the first day that the stamp could be used. (The first-ever first-day cover would be one bearing a Penny Black canceled on May 6, 1840.)

Collecting first-day covers is now a popular part of stamp collecting. Envelopes specially printed with a design relevant to the stamp issue are produced by post offices and private manufacturers. These covers often contain a card that provides information about the stamp issue. Special postmarks with pictorial designs are also produced to cancel the stamps.

Similar in appearance to first-day covers are those produced to mark a special event. They differ in that the stamps are not always canceled on the first day of issue. Another item much like the first-day cover is the maximum card (Maxicard), a picture postcard with a design related to that of a stamp. The stamp is stuck on the picture side of the card and canceled with an appropriate postmark.

All these items can be bought complete from dealers. However, many collectors like to stick the stamps on and address the envelopes themselves, either to mail (for cancellation), or to have a special postmark applied by the post office. The U.S. Postal Service publishes a *Postal Bulletin* that contains information on first-day covers. This information is also displayed in most post offices. Subscription details can be obtained from: Superintendent of Documents, U.S. Government Printing Office, 710 North Capitol Street NE, Washington, D.C. 20402-3238.

DISPLAYING COVERS
Special albums are available for storing a collection of covers or postcards. These contain pages of transparent pockets, one or two to a page, into which the covers are slipped. The pockets usually contain a thin card, and the covers are mounted, using the

A selection of first-day covers with (top) a special event cover and (bottom left) a Maxicard.

transparent corners used to mount photographs, on either side—thus, each pocket will hold two covers. Pockets are available with an opening at the side or the top; the top-opening type is preferable because it will not let a loose cover fall into the album's binding mechanism.

PREPARING FIRST-DAY COVERS

When preparing first-day covers, don't stick the stamps too near the envelope's edge, and make sure that they are straight and neat. The postmark will be seen easily if you place the stamps in a row across the top of the envelope rather than in a block.

When sticking the stamps down, leave plenty of room for the address. A typewritten address looks much neater than one written by hand; better still are small pre-printed self-adhesive address labels.

Special albums with clear plastic pockets are available to protect your covers and cards.

POSTMARKS

Any mark applied to an item sent through the mail during the course of its journey is a postmark. Such marks may be handwritten or applied by handstamp or machine. They may show the type of service paid for, how the item was sent, the route taken, the time and place of mailing, charges to be paid, or other special instructions. The best-known type of postmark gives the time and place of mailing.

EARLY POSTMARKS

Postmarks reveal the history and development of the postal service. The earliest British date stamp was devised by Henry Bishop in 1661. It showed the day and month of mailing and was introduced to answer complaints about delays in the mail. In 1680 William Dockwra's London Penny Post used a triangular mark showing that postage had been paid.

There are some postmarks that prevent a stamp being reused. They are known as cancellations. The first of them was the so-called Maltese Cross used on the British Penny Black in 1840. It gave no indication of time or place of mailing, which was applied by a separate handstamp on the back of the letter.

A Dockwra mark
(left). Below is a
letter from 1702
with a Bishop mark.

Early stamps from Afghanistan were canceled by being torn (below).

Argentine stamps with cancellations in pen (above).

Pre-canceled stamps from France, the U.S., and Belgium (below).

UNUSUAL POSTMARKS

There are many other types of postmarks used by postal administrations. Postmarks can indicate that there is extra postage to pay, give reasons for delay or damage, show why a letter was undeliverable, or convey numerous other types of information. In France and some other countries, stamps are issued with a postmark already printed on them. Known as pre-cancels, these stamps are used for sending bulk quantities of mail.

The Maltese Cross cancel was first in red. It was later changed to black.

MODERN CANCELLATIONS

Today, many date-stamp and cancellation devices are combined. The cancellation takes the form of lines or an advertising slogan. Pictorial cancellations are often produced for special occasions such as the first day of a stamp issue, an exhibition, an anniversary, or some other important event. Such postmarks should not be overlooked by topical collectors. They can make an interesting and unusual addition to a topical collection.

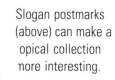

Slogan postmarks (above) can make a topical collection more interesting.

Look for covers (top and center) with interesting markings. Special postmarks (above) are produced to mark many events.

Heavily postmarked stamps like these (left) should not be included in your collection.

METER MARKS

Meter marks are applied by machines operated by private users licensed by a post office. They combine a "stamp," date stamp, and often an advertising slogan. Similar in appearance are automatic stamps (see page 31), such as the French and Norwegian ones below.

OVERPRINTS

An inscription or some other feature added to the design side of a stamp is known as an overprint. There are many reasons why a stamp might be overprinted. For example, a country that has no stamps of its own may use those of another country. The first stamps issued by the island of Cyprus were produced by overprinting those of Great Britain. A country's stamps may also be overprinted to indicate a change of name or status.

SPECIAL ISSUES

Overprinting can be used to produce special stamp issues. This may change an everyday stamp into one for official use only, or into a commemorative issue. Commemorative stamps themselves are often overprinted to enhance their original purpose. For example stamps issued to mark the Olympic Games or World Cups are often overprinted with the names of some of the winning athletes and teams.

Fijian stamps have been overprinted for the New Hebrides (above). The overprint is missing from the top stamp.

This overprint publicized a disastrous hurricane in British Honduras (now Belize). Sales of the stamps raised funds for relief work.

These overprints were for an event for which there was not time to design a stamp (above left), and for making U.S. stamps valid in the Panama Canal zone (above right).

This football stamp (left) was overprinted for the French Cup. The Olympic Games overprints (above and right) name event winners.

When the Central African Republic became an empire, the existing stamps (left) were overprinted with the new name.

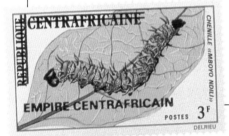

SECURITY

Stamps may be overprinted for security purposes. This is often done by companies in order to prevent theft, but has also been carried out by postal authorities. Stamps are sometimes perforated with an initial or a design for the same reason: these are known as *perfins*. In 1934, Greek letters were included in an airmail overprint on a Macao stamp in order to make forgery difficult.

SURCHARGES

Overprints that include a change of value are known as surcharges. There are many reasons for making surcharges. Stamps may be surcharged because of a shortage of those of a particular value, perhaps because a new printing has been delayed, or because there has been an increase in postal rates. Sometimes, changes of value are made to use up unwanted stocks of old stamps.

Several British Commonwealth countries surcharged existing stamps when they changed to a new decimal currency (see page 28). Surcharges may also be used to raise funds to aid a sudden emergency.

SPECIMENS

Overprinting can also be used to prevent a stamp from being used for postal purposes. Stamps are very often overprinted with the words "canceled" or "specimen" (or their foreign equivalent) when they are used for publicity purposes, or when they are distributed to other postal authorities as a reference.

MAKESHIFT OVERPRINTS

Overprints and surcharges are often applied in emergencies by handstamps or typeset printing plates. This frequently results in errors such as missing letters and inverted type. They can also be handwritten or typed, though this does not happen very often.

This stamp from Newfoundland has a handwritten overprinting that includes the postmaster's initials. The overprinted stamp was intended for use on a pioneering transatlantic flight in 1919.

Commemorative (above left) and charity (above right) surcharges. The Newfoundland stamp has the surcharge inverted.

The three definitive stamps from Gambia, the Netherlands, and Zambia (above) have surcharges changing their value. The Gambian stamp has a double surcharge.

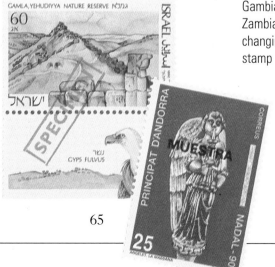

An Israeli stamp overprinted "specimen" (far left), and an Andorran one with the Spanish equivalent, "Muestra" (left).

CINDERELLAS

There are many items that look like postage stamps but that cannot be found in most stamp catalogs. Some, though performing a limited postal service, have not been issued by a government postal authority. Others are not postage stamps at all. These items are called *Cinderellas*.

PRIVATE MAIL SERVICES
Probably the most popular of these Cinderellas are those issued by private companies or local authorities. Produced in limited numbers, they are difficult to find, especially ones used on covers. Stamps produced by British railway companies that ran trains before British Rail are much sought after. Some are still issued in Great Britain by many small railway companies. These railway stamps paid for the carriage of mail on the railway's route. Airline and bus companies have issued similar items.

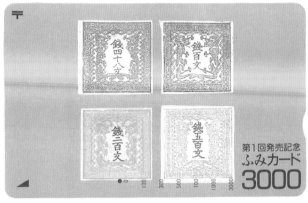

A Japanese card for buying stamps (above). A British telephone-bill savings stamp and telegraph stamp (left).

Bogus stamps from the non-existent territories of Occussi Ambeno (left) and Sedang (below).

A British-railway letter stamp (left) and a cover carried on Great Britain's Talyllyn Railway (below).

REVENUES

Revenue stamps, issued to collect government taxes and duties, are also widely collected, especially in the U.S. A variety particularly popular with many American collectors are the stamps permitting duck hunting. Known as "duck stamps" because their attractive designs depict species of ducks, they have a strong following.

MISCELLANY

Other Cinderella items are phantom, or bogus, stamps (produced by eccentric people for places that do not exist, sometimes to sell to collectors); Christmas seals; postal labels such as those used for airmail or registration purposes; exhibition and other advertising and commemorative labels; and savings stamps—in fact, just about anything that looks like a stamp!

Although many Cinderella items can make unusual additions to a standard stamp collection, they can also be collected in their own right. There is even a special society—the Cinderella Stamp Club—devoted to the study of these non-postal stamps.

Two "duck stamps." The hunter's signature "cancels" the stamps and makes the hunting permit valid.

Patriotic stamplike labels from Finland and Denmark (right).

Revenue stamps from Belgium (top), Hong Kong (center), and Malta, the latter being an overprinted postage stamp.

A Zimbabwe airport departure-fee stamp (above) valued in U.S. dollars.

These "local" stamps, right, are from the Norwegian island of Spitzbergen, from Clipperton Island in the north Pacific, and from Lundy in the English Channel.

CHRISTMAS MAIL

In Great Britain, a recent addition to Cinderella philately are the stamps of many charity postal services operated at Christmastime. Often organized by Scout groups, these local services carry Christmas cards at a reduced rate. Special stamps, postmarks, and covers are often produced for them.

STAMP CLUBS

Joining a stamp club or philatelic society allows you to meet others with the same hobby and helps you learn more about philately. Most clubs organize a program of events that includes visiting speakers, members' displays, competitions, and opportunities to swap and buy stamps. Many arrange visits to exhibitions or hold their own. Some publish a newsletter keeping members in touch.

TYPES OF CLUB

Many schools run stamp clubs. If yours has one, you should join it. You could help plan the club's activities, and maybe organize an auction! Most large towns also have a philatelic society. Although these are mainly for adults, some have a junior section.

The more experienced and expert collector may wish to join a specialist society devoted to the stamps of a particular country, area, or topic. There are also countrywide societies. Some useful addresses are listed on the next page.

If you have a particular interest in the stamps of another country, why not join one of their stamp clubs? In many countries the post office organizes a junior stamp club. Some have even issued stamps designed by the club's members.

Sorting and soaking stamps at a stamp-club meeting can be lots of fun.

BENJAMIN FRANKLIN STAMP CLUBS (BFSCs)

The U.S. Postal Service sponsors the Benjamin Franklin Stamp Clubs (BFSCs). There are 42,000 of them nationwide, run by public and private schools, libraries, Boy Scout troops, and adult stamp clubs. Members receive a *Treasury of Stamps* album and an *Introduction to Stamp Collecting* booklet, and films are available on a loan basis from the Postal Service. If you wish to start a BFSC in your school or area, have a teacher or other adult contact your local post office or write to: Ben Franklin Stamp Club Coordinator, U.S. Postal Service, P.O. Box 449994, Kansas City, Missouri 64144-9994.

FINDING A CLUB

Your local library will usually be able to tell you if there is a stamp club in your area. Your library is also a good source of information about stamp collecting, with books and catalogs often available for loan or reference. Many libraries have one or more monthly stamp magazines to use for reference.

The post offices of many countries sponsor stamp clubs. For example, in Guernsey, an island off the coast of France, the post office sponsors a First Class Club that offers an exciting starter package.

USEFUL ADDRESSES

You can belong to stamp clubs both in the U.S. and throughout the world. Here are some useful addresses.

United States: The Junior Philatelists of America, P.O. Box 701010, San Antonio, Texas 78270; American Philatelic Society, P.O. Box 8000, State College, Pennsylvania 16803; Philatelic Foundation, 21 East 40th Street, New York, New York 10016.

Canada: Canada Post's club for young stamp collectors is The Stamp Travellers Club, Canada Post Corporation, Antigonish, Nova Scotia, Canada B2G 2R8.

Great Britain: The National Philatelic Society and the British Philatelic Federation, both at 107 Charterhouse Street, London, Great Britian EC1M 6PT.

Guernsey: First-Class Stamp Club, Guernsey Post Office, Postal Headquarters, Guernsey, Channel Islands.

New Zealand: New Zealand Post produces a free bulletin, *Focus*, for collectors of all ages. Send your name and address with a request to be placed on the mailing list to: Basil Umuroa, Manager, Philatelic Bureau, New Zealand Post Ltd, Private Bag, Wanganui, New Zealand.

Australia: The Australian Post Office produces a magazine, *The Stamp Explorer*, for young collectors. It is available from Reply Paid, *Stamp Explorer*, P.O. Box 511, South Melbourne, Victoria 3205, Australia.

FOREIGN ALPHABETS

One of the pleasures of collecting stamps comes from the glimpse they give of life in foreign lands. You will soon notice that many countries use different names from those we use. Ireland, for example, is *Eire*; Switzerland calls itself *Helvetia*. Some countries do not even use the same alphabet that we use.

GREEK AND CYRILLIC

Most countries in Europe, as well as many elsewhere, use the Latin alphabet—the type of letters used in this book. Two other alphabets are also used on stamps in Europe, however, and both contain letters similar to those in the Latin alphabet, as well as some that are not so familiar.

The first of these is Greek, which may be found on the stamps of Greece and Cyprus. The name on Greek stamps translates as *Ellas*, and a Latin alphabet equivalent of this—*Hellas*—appears on modern Greek stamps.

The three stamps above left, from Mongolia, the former USSR, and Yugoslavia, have Cyrillic inscriptions. The other two stamps are from Greece.

The second alphabet is Cyrillic, an adaptation of Greek. You'll find this alphabet used on the stamps of what was the USSR (Union of Soviet Socialist Republics—Russia in catalogs): the Cyrillic looks like the letters *CCCP*. You will also find Cyrillic used on stamps from Bulgaria, Mongolia, and Yugoslavia.

ALPHABETS OF THE WORLD

αβßγδεζηθικλμνξπορσςτυφφχψω
ΑΒΓΔΕΖΗΘΙΚΛΜΝΞΠΟΡΣΤΥΦΧ
ΨΩ 1234567890 .,:;!?

Οἱ πρῶτες ἐκδώσεις ἑλληνικῶν κειμένων ἔγιναν στό τυπο είο τοῦ Ἄλδου Μανουτίου στή Βενετία. Ἀπο τό 1494 ὡς τό

Greek

абвгдежзийклмнопрстуфхцчшщъыьэ
юя АБВГДЕЖЗИЙКЛМНОПРСТУФХ
ЦЧШЩЪЫЬЭЮЯ 1234567890 .,:;!?

Азот является одним из главных элементов входящих в состав ве ществ, сбразующих живое тело растений и животных. В процесса

Cyrillic

ابتتثجحخدذرزسشصضطظعغففقكلمنهوىلا
١٢٣٤٥٦٧٨٩٠

فجهاز السي آر ترونيك ٢٠٠ لايعتمد في تصويره لاشكال الحروف ، على عدسات أو مرايا أو قطع ميكانيكية متحركة

Arabic

किसी जाति के जीवन में उसके द्वारा प्रयुक्त शब्दों का अत्यंत महत्त्वपूर्ण स्थान है । आवश्यकता तथा स्थिति के अनुसार इन प्रयुक्त शब्दों का आगम

Indian

OTHER ALPHABETS

Arabic script can be found on stamps from many places—from Mauritania in Africa to Afghanistan in Asia. Fortunately, most of these stamps also carry a Latin alphabet (our alphabet) version of their country name, making identification easier. So, too, do the stamps of Ethiopia, Israel, India, and other countries that have alphabets other than ours.

The same cannot be said for many stamps of China, Japan, and Korea, whose different characters often appear very similar to Western eyes. Modern stamps from these countries do often carry a Latin alphabet version of their name—*Nippon*, for example, shows that a stamp is from Japan. The items shown on these pages should help you to sort out earlier stamps from these countries.

Stamps with Arabic (right) and Hebrew (far right) scripts. The stamp below is from South Korea.

Stamps from India are bilingual.

This Japanese stamp can be identified by the chrysanthemum symbol.

A stamp from the Himalayan kingdom of Bhutan.

A stamp from Communist China (left) and two from Taiwan (above). Note the 中 character.

STAMPS WITHOUT NAMES

When Great Britain issued the Penny Black in 1840, there was no need for the country name to be on it, as no other countries had stamps. Many other early stamps were also issued without a country name. This still continues today on British stamps, though each bears the reigning monarch's head as a means of identification.

Some countries are identified by their initials. USA, for United States of America, is well known; other examples include RSA (Republic of South Africa), SWA (South West Africa, now Namibia), DDR (Deutsche Demokratische Republik, better known as the former East Germany), and KSA (Kingdom of Saudi Arabia). Stamps from Saudi Arabia now carry the country's emblem—a palm tree and crossed scimitars—as a symbol of recognition.

A British stamp showing King George VI.

A greetings stamp from the United States.

The palm tree emblem identifies this Saudi Arabian stamp.

A stamp from the former German Democratic Republic (DDR).

British stamps have never had a country name. They are identified by the monarch's head.

STAMP MAPS

Unless you are very good at geography, or have traveled a lot, you probably will not know the names of or where to find all the stamp-issuing countries of the world. The maps provided here can be used with catalogs and printed stamp albums to help organize your collection. The maps show present-day stamp-issuing countries. Also, where the name in English is significantly different from the name in a country's own language, the maps show that country's name as it appears on its stamps. The names in parentheses are names used previously by those countries.

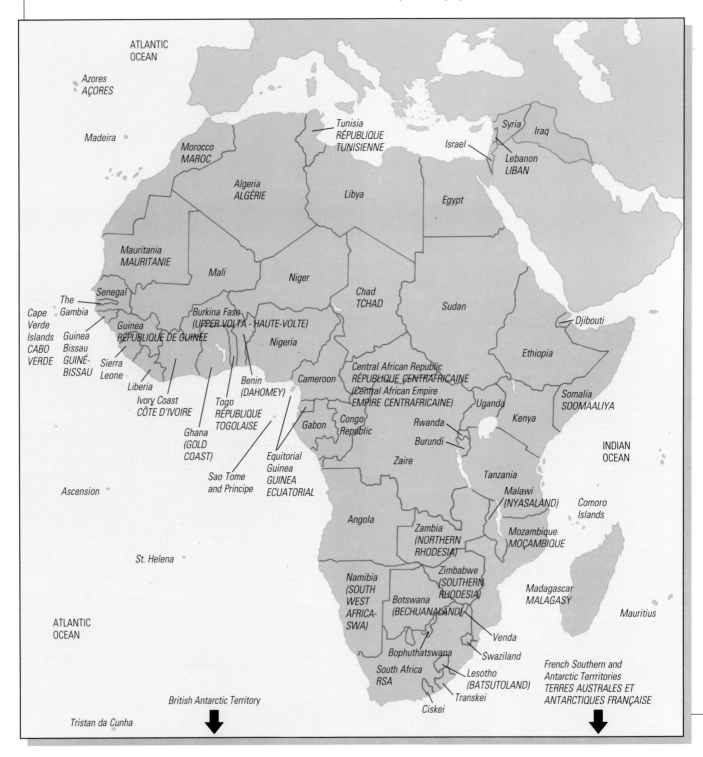

ATLANTIC OCEAN

Azores
AÇORES

Madeira

Tunisia
RÉPUBLIQUE
TUNISIENNE

Syria   Iraq

Israel

Lebanon
LIBAN

Morocco
MAROC

Algeria
ALGÉRIE

Libya

Egypt

Mauritania
MAURITANIE

Mali

Niger

Chad
TCHAD

Sudan

Djibouti

The
Senegal   Gambia

Cape
Verde
Islands
CABO
VERDE

Guinea
Bissau
GUINÉ-
BISSAU

Guinea
RÉPUBLIQUE DE GUINÉE

Burkina Faso
(UPPER VOLTA - HAUTE-VOLTE)

Nigeria

Ethiopia

Sierra
Leone

Liberia

Ivory Coast
CÔTE D'IVOIRE

Togo
RÉPUBLIQUE
TOGOLAISE

Ghana
(GOLD
COAST)

Benin
(DAHOMEY)

Cameroon

Central African Republic
RÉPUBLIQUE CENTRAFRICAINE
(Central African Empire
EMPIRE CENTRAFRICAINE)

Uganda

Somalia
SOOMAALIYA

Kenya

Gabon

Congo
Republic

Rwanda

Burundi

Equitorial
Guinea
GUINEA
ECUATORIAL

Sao Tome
and Principe

Zaire

Tanzania

INDIAN
OCEAN

Ascension

St. Helena

Angola

Malawi
(NYASALAND)

Comoro
Islands

Zambia
(NORTHERN
RHODESIA)

Mozambique
MOÇAMBIQUE

Namibia
(SOUTH
WEST
AFRICA-
SWA)

Zimbabwe
(SOUTHERN
RHODESIA)

Botswana
(BECHUANALAND)

Madagascar
MALAGASY

Mauritius

ATLANTIC
OCEAN

Venda

Bophuthatswana

Swaziland

South Africa
RSA

Lesotho
(BATSUTOLAND)

Transkei

Ciskei

French Southern and
Antarctic Terrritories
TERRES AUSTRALES ET
ANTARCTIQUES FRANÇAISE

British Antarctic Territory

Tristan da Cunha

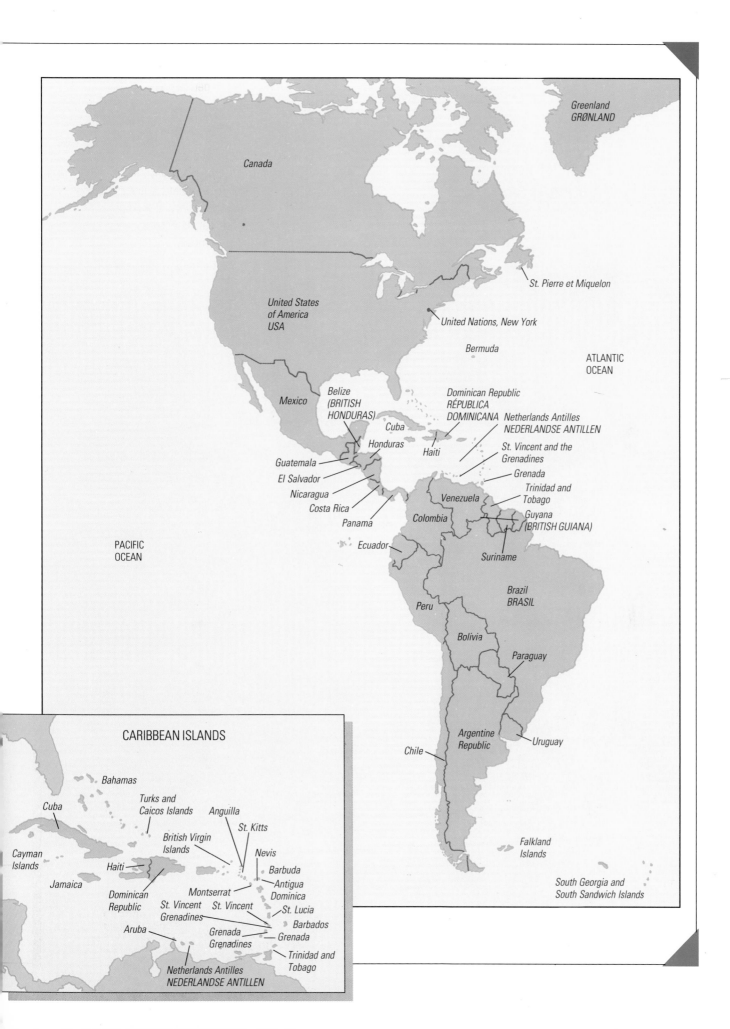

Greenland
GRØNLAND

Canada

St. Pierre et Miquelon

United States
of America
USA

United Nations, New York

Bermuda

ATLANTIC
OCEAN

Belize
(BRITISH
HONDURAS)

Mexico

Cuba

Dominican Republic
RÉPUBLICA
DOMINICANA

Netherlands Antilles
NEDERLANDSE ANTILLEN

Honduras

Haiti

St. Vincent and the
Grenadines

Guatemala

Grenada

El Salvador

Trinidad and
Tobago

Nicaragua

Venezuela

Costa Rica

Guyana
(BRITISH GUIANA)

Panama

Colombia

Suriname

PACIFIC
OCEAN

Ecuador

Brazil
BRASIL

Peru

Bolivia

Paraguay

Argentine
Republic

Uruguay

Chile

Falkland
Islands

South Georgia and
South Sandwich Islands

CARIBBEAN ISLANDS

Bahamas

Cuba

Turks and
Caicos Islands

Anguilla

St. Kitts

British Virgin
Islands

Nevis

Cayman
Islands

Haiti

Barbuda

Jamaica

Antigua

Dominican
Republic

Montserrat

Dominica

St. Vincent
Grenadines

St. Vincent

St. Lucia

Aruba

Grenada
Grenadines

Barbados

Grenada

Trinidad and
Tobago

Netherlands Antilles
NEDERLANDSE ANTILLEN

ATLANTIC
OCEAN

Iceland
ISLAND

Faroe Islands
FØROYAR

Sweden
SVERIGE

Finland
SUOMI FINLAND

Åland
Islands

Norway
NORGE
or NOREG

Isle
of Man

Denmark
DANMARK

Estonia
EESTI

Latvia
LATVIJA

Russia
(Soviet Union—CCCP)

Netherlands
NEDERLAND

Lithuania
LIETUVA

Ireland
EIRE

Belgium
BELGIQUE
BELGIË

Great
Britain

Germany
DEUTSCHE BUNDESPOST
(DEUTSCHE POST or
DEUTSCHES
REICH to 1949)

Poland
POLSKA

Belarus

Alderney

Guernsey

Jersey

Luxembourg

(East Germany -
DDR)

Czechoslovakia
CESKOSLOVENSKO

France
RÉPUBLIQUE FRANÇAISE

United Nations, Vienna
VEREINTE NATIONEN

Ukraine

Liechtenstein

Switzerland
HELVETIA

Austria
ÖSTERREICH

Hungary
MAGYARORZAG
[MAGYAR POSTA]

United Nations,
Geneva
NATIONS UNIES

Italy
ITALIA

Rumania
ROMANA

Monaco

Yugoslavia
JUGOSLAVIJA

Spain
ESPAÑA

Andorra
[French]
POSTES

San Marino

Bulgaria
НРЪЪЛАРИЯ

Andorra
[Spanish]
CORREOS

Vatican City
POSTE
VATICANE

Turkey
TÜRKIYE

Portugal

Gibraltar

Albania
SHQIPERIA

Malta

Greece
ΕΛΛΑΣ/HELLAS

MEDITERRANEAN SEA

Cyprus
[Republic]

Cyprus [Turkish]
KUZEY KIBRIS
TÜRK
CUMHURIYETI

74

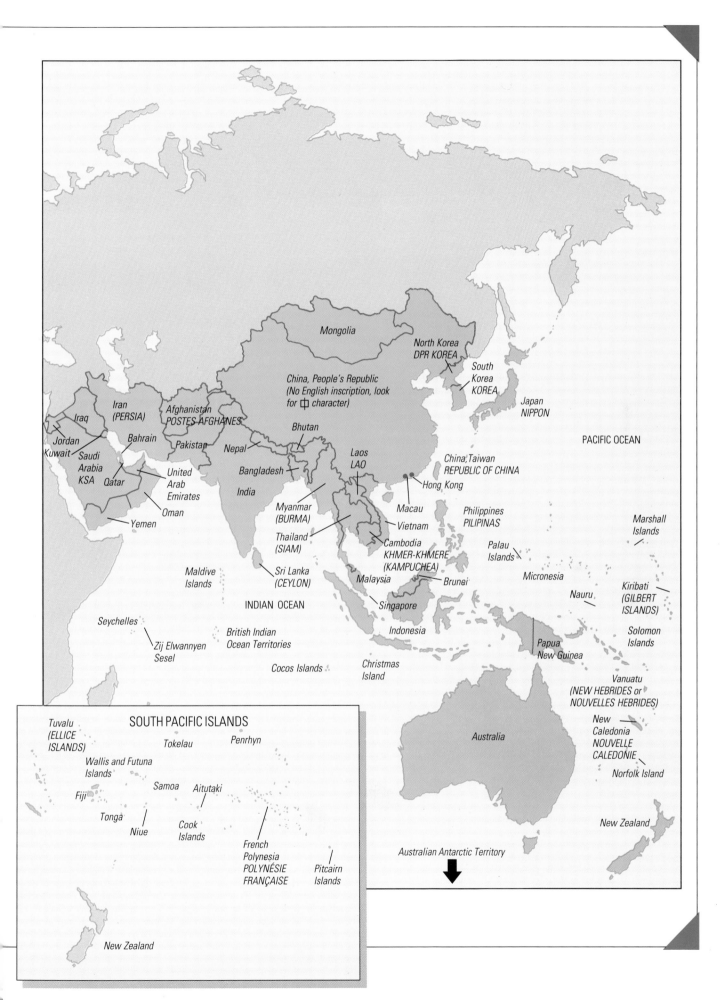

Mongolia

North Korea
DPR KOREA

South
Korea
KOREA

China, People's Republic
(No English inscription, look
for 中 character)

Japan
NIPPON

PACIFIC OCEAN

Iran
(PERSIA)

Afghanistan
POSTES AFGHANES

Iraq

Jordan
Kuwait

Bahrain

Saudi
Arabia
KSA

Qatar

United
Arab
Emirates

Oman

Yemen

Pakistan

Nepal

Bhutan

Bangladesh

India

Myanmar
(BURMA)

Thailand
(SIAM)

Laos
LAO

China, Taiwan
REPUBLIC OF CHINA

Hong Kong

Macau

Vietnam

Cambodia
KHMER-KHMERE
(KAMPUCHEA)

Philippines
PILIPINAS

Marshall
Islands

Palau
Islands

Micronesia

Nauru

Kiribati
(GILBERT
ISLANDS)

Maldive
Islands

Sri Lanka
(CEYLON)

Malaysia

Singapore

Brunei

Solomon
Islands

INDIAN OCEAN

Indonesia

Seychelles

Zij Elwannyen
Sesel

British Indian
Ocean Territories

Cocos Islands

Christmas
Island

Papua
New Guinea

Vanuatu
(NEW HEBRIDES or
NOUVELLES HEBRIDES)

New
Caledonia
NOUVELLE
CALEDONIE

Norfolk Island

Australia

New Zealand

Australian Antarctic Territory

SOUTH PACIFIC ISLANDS

Tuvalu
(ELLICE
ISLANDS)

Tokelau

Penrhyn

Wallis and Futuna
Islands

Samoa

Aitutaki

Fiji

Tonga

Niue

Cook
Islands

French
Polynesia
POLYNÉSIE
FRANÇAISE

Pitcairn
Islands

New Zealand

INDEX